Who doesn't like a smile? Whether it's from a child or your best friend, everyone loves a smile. *Wake Up Smiling* by Audrey Meisner is a wonderful book. You might just *Wake Up Smiling* as a lifelong habit after reading through this daily devotional. Allow Audrey to take you by the hand and show you her discoveries. You'll learn the secrets of maintaining your peace no matter what surrounds you and how to keep your Joy-Light switched on. And when people ask you, "Why do you wake up smiling?" tell them about this book! You better buy a few, because you'll want to share it with your friends. Enjoy the next forty days of your joyous journey into finding your smile again!

—Dr. Brian Simmons, The Passion Translation Project

It's been over twelve years since we personally witnessed Audrey experience a dramatic breakthrough when she completely received the beautiful forgiveness of Jesus. It was tangible and real. Since that moment when she "threw off" the cloak of shame, she hasn't looked back. We prayed for her that night in her parents' living room, and since then we have seen her walk in an authority of joy and freedom that is contagious and miraculous. You can't help but smile and receive practical strategy as you follow the journey to happiness that Audrey has walked and laid out here in this book. Read every page of *Wake Up Smiling*. It will help you see how much you were created for new levels of breakthrough!

—Dr. Don and Mary Colbert,
New York Times best-selling authors

Wake Up Smiling is a book every person should read. The reason this book is so powerful is because I know this about Audrey Meisner. She is completely authentic. Her words emerge from a life of applying God's truth. There's nothing theoretical in her teaching. She is completely transparent. For the benefit of others, she never holds back. She is a true Jesus girl who bases her every belief in the life, teaching, death, burial, and resurrection of the Lord Jesus.

—James B. Richards, PhD, ThD

Audrey Meisner is by nature a happy, joyful person. But that's not what qualifies her to write this book. Audrey has walked through deep valleys of grief, heartbreak, and impossible circumstances, only to emerge with profound passion and a firmer grasp of God's great love for her and for others (like you). This is not a surfacey book about the benefits of smiling (although, Audrey definitely points out the benefits of smiling). This is an honest look at what hinders our joy and why it matters. Do you believe it's possible to embrace life with a heart of expectancy and faith? Do you want to wake up smiling because you're someone Jesus loves and sings over? Read this book. It's like a cup of cool water: good for the heart and good for the soul.

—Susie Larson, national speaker, talk-radio host, and author of *Your Powerful Prayers*

Audrey's writing and her ministry are real, raw, and honest. The truths in her book, *Wake Up Smiling*, will help others held in captivity find their freedom. The healing in her journey with God will give so many their own pathways. If you are looking to be challenged and set free, this book is for you!

—MATTHEW AND CAROLINE BARNETT,
founders of the Dream Center, Los Angeles, CA

Practical and powerful, *Wake up Smiling* reflects Audrey's authenticity and zest for life. Each chapter is packed with doable strategies for joyful living. Audrey inspires us to allow the peace of God to rule in our hearts—no matter the circumstances. What a timely message for a weary world! This is the type of book that you will turn to again and again for encouragement and renewed hope.

—DEBORAH SMITH PEGUES, best-selling author
of *30 Days to Taming Your Tongue*

Audrey's book, *Wake Up Smiling*, is not just a daily devotional. It is a training manual with practical steps to living a hope-filled life. She leaves nothing hidden as she shares with vulnerability and openness about her own journey to personal victory. She combines her story with biblical truth to make this a very powerful read. We highly recommend diving into this book and letting your life be impacted daily by the truth of her message. As Audrey says, "Let's make a choice to line up with heaven and live in hope everyday."

—STEVE AND WENDY BACKLUND, Bethel Church,
Redding, CA, and founders of Igniting Hope Ministries

Anyone who meets Audrey is instantly caught up in her zest for life, her love for Jesus, and the contagious joy she emanates. So I read her new book, *Wake Up Smiling*, with great anticipation, knowing I would be encouraged. But I found so much more. In this book she shares hard-earned wisdom that is made easily accessible and can be practically applied. Her passion will inspire you, and her story of grace will disarm you from any dread of the future so that every day you can confidently *Wake up Smiling*.

—JUDITH CRIST, Lead Pastor, Hillsong, Phoenix

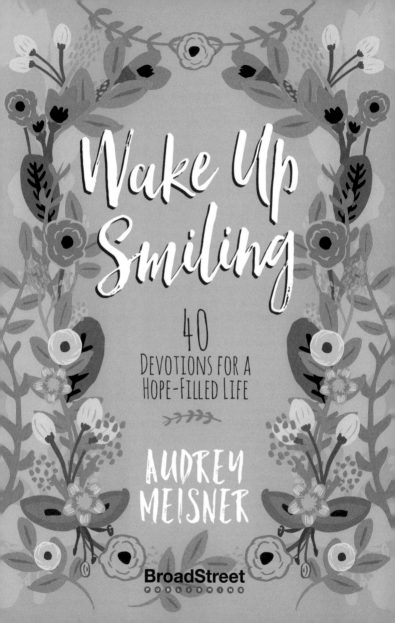

Wake Up Smiling

40
Devotions for a
Hope-Filled Life

Audrey Meisner

BroadStreet
PUBLISHING

BroadStreet Publishing Group, LLC
Racine, Wisconsin, USA
BroadStreetPublishing.com

Wake Up Smiling: 40 Devotions for a Hope-Filled Life

Copyright © 2017 Audrey Meisner

ISBN-13: 978-1-4245-5380-8 (hardcover)
ISBN-13: 978-1-4245-5381-5 (e-book)

Unless otherwise indicated, all Scripture quotations are taken from the Holy Bible, New Living Translation, copyright © 1996, 2004, 2007, 2013, 2015 by Tyndale House Foundation. Used by permission of Tyndale House Publishers, Inc., Carol Stream, Illinois 60188. All rights reserved. Scripture quotations marked NIV are taken from the Holy Bible, New International Version®, NIV®. Copyright © 1973, 1978, 1984, 2011 by Biblica, Inc.™ Used by permission of Zondervan. All rights reserved worldwide. www.zondervan.com The "NIV" and "New International Version" are trademarks registered in the United States Patent and Trademark Office by Biblica, Inc.™ Scripture quotations marked TPT are from The Passion Translation®, copyright © 2014, 2015. Used by permission of BroadStreet Publishing Group, LLC, Racine, Wisconsin, USA. All rights reserved. ThePassionTranslation.com. Scripture quotations marked VOICE are taken from The Voice™. Copyright © 2008 by Ecclesia Bible Society. Used by permission. All rights reserved. Scripture quotations marked NKJV are taken from the New King James Version®. Copyright © 1982 by Thomas Nelson. Used by permission. All rights reserved. Scripture quotations marked AMPCE are taken from the Amplified Bible, Copyright © 1954, 1958, 1962, 1964, 1965, 1987 by The Lockman Foundation. Used by permission.

Stock or custom editions of BroadStreet Publishing titles may be purchased in bulk for educational, business, ministry, fundraising, or sales promotional use. For information, please e-mail info@broadstreetpublishing.com.

Art direction by David Meisner
Cover design by Chris Garborg, GarborgDesign.com
Interior design and typeset by Katherine Lloyd, theDESKonline.com

Printed in China
17 18 19 20 5 4 3 2 1

To my dad who has the widest smile,

the most infectious joy,

and the best made-up morning songs.

How can a girl not wake up smiling

with a dad like you?

Contents

Our Lives Tell a Story 11

Fun Facts about Smiling 19

PART ONE: *The Happy Me*

Day 1   Happy People 24

Day 2   Peace Regained. 27

Day 3   A Key to Happiness 30

Day 4   Transferring Trust 33

Day 5   An Invitation to Happiness. 36

Day 6   Peace No Matter the Season. 39

Day 7   Happy Like a Child. 42

Day 8   Pain as a Gateway to Joy 46

Day 9   Keeping Joy amid Sorrow. 49

Day 10   Monuments of Joy 52

PART TWO: *The Invisible Me*

Day 11   Deepest Craving. 58

Day 12   More than Meets the Eye 62

Day 13   All the Days of My Life 65

Day 14   The Substance of Spirit 68

Day 15   Understanding Spirit Substance 72

Day 16   Aligned with Heaven and Led by the Spirit 76

Day 17   The Earthly Things Seem So Real 80

Day 18   The Things That Lurk. 84

Day 19 What Do I Look Like?. 87

Day 20 Spiritual Eyes. 91

PART THREE: *The Surrendered Me*

Day 21 My Happy Place 98

Day 22 Aligned for an Open Heaven 102

Day 23 Who's Driving?. 105

Day 24 Surrendering My Mind 108

Day 25 Surrendering My Will. 111

Day 26 Surrendering My Emotions 114

Day 27 Surrendering My Stuff. 118

Day 28 Surrendering My Appetites. 121

Day 29 Surrendering My Opinions 124

Day 30 Surrendering My Idea of Success. 128

PART FOUR: *The Hope-Filled Me*

Day 31 A Recipe for Hope 134

Day 32 Living above the Hope Line 138

Day 33 The Weight of Anxiety and Concerns. 142

Day 34 The Weight of Unanswered Prayer 146

Day 35 The Weight of an Offense 150

Day 36 The Weight of Regrets, Guilt, and Secrets 153

Day 37 The Truth about Wanting to Give Up 157

Day 38 The Truth about Hard Times 161

Day 39 Oh, to Be a Prisoner 165

Day 40 Hope for True Rest. 169

Acknowledgments 173

About the Author 175

Our Lives Tell a Story

My earliest memory is twirling around alone in my treehouse, singing "Hosanna, hosanna, hosanna to the King of Kings!" I grew up with normal childhood challenges but continuously experienced God as my best friend. As the baby of the family, I thrived on love and attention, and being funny and silly brought me plenty of both. I've always loved a good party—and to be the life of the party.

Laughing my way through life got me through full-time ministry, three kids, and pioneering a church with my dreamy husband. But that last endeavor also ended every dream and launched the beginning of a horrific nightmare. The responsibility involved was overwhelming, the lack of success began to define me, and my enthusiastic zest for life started dying fast. Determined to push through, I buried my loneliness, disappointment, and sheer exhaustion.

My escape was laughter, and my desperation led me to search out a friend who had nothing to do with responsibility. Our laughter eased my pain, and because he was so much younger, I believed I could break the rules of opposite-sex relationships. I felt in control and experienced welcome relief. But then the friendship grew into a physical relationship, and I rationalized the e-mails, the attachment, and the compromise. "*That* Audrey" was winning—the desperate Audrey who suffered silent pain, gasping for breath.

The path of adultery led to confusion, chaos, secrets, and shame. Not a pretty picture, and after three weeks I couldn't live another day in my dual lifestyle. I ended the relationship and confessed to my husband, Bob. Not knowing what to do, we reached out for help, and God began a rescue plan for our lives and our marriage. Our pain was intense yet separate, but we prayed together, cried together, got mad together, and determined to find out what kind of dysfunction had led us to such a sorry state.

The plot thickened when we learned I was pregnant as a result of the affair. The baby would be biracial and would not look like the rest of our family. The enemy whispered into my fragile heart, *You're going to be known for the rest of your life for the most stupid and selfish thing you have ever done. Your kids are going to be messed up because of your mistake. You're disqualified from ministry, and you never ever deserve to laugh and enjoy life again.*

I called an abortion clinic and found out I could place an order for ten little pills that would "take care of my problem." I fell to my knees and cried out to God, "I can't abort this baby, but God, if you love me, you will take this from me." I begged Him for a miscarriage. Even now, years later, I get emotional as I write this, because out of love for me, God did *not* answer that prayer. Instead, He met me in my pain and healed my broken heart.

My healing took years, but it was worth every tear I shed.

Jesus comes to heal the broken-hearted. Bob and I have written books together that chronicle our journey of how God rescued us from the darkest season of our life, and, in His mercy and grace, developed character in our lives and poured His favor and reward on our family. One of the greatest gifts He has given me is His righteousness. Let me explain.

During the pregnancy, I asked God to help me hate what I had done. I figured that if I hated the sin, I wouldn't do it again. If only I could be righteous enough. If only I could turn back the clock and make the right choices. If only I could have avoided all this pain I caused my husband, my family, and myself. But that's not the way life works.

Our marriage toiled through rough terrain during the pregnancy. We had good days and bad days, and then on one of the scariest days of my life, October 7, 2001, we went to the hospital and I gave birth to a teeny-tiny black-haired boy. Bob looked into my eyes and announced that he wanted to name this little boy Robert, after himself. He chose the name Theodore as his middle name, declaring its meaning of "divine gift," and truly, that is exactly what Robert has been to our family. Our little guy was not an accident, a mistake, or the result of a sexual affair; he is a gift straight from heaven.

Our first book, *Marriage Under Cover*, gives a transparent account of the whole story, and is full of hope and healing for marriages. Now, every one of our four children is experiencing God's love every day, and our creed is "We are a family who loves God intimately, each other openly, and the world radically." I could not be more thankful for God's redeeming love and for my husband, Bob, who has loved me unconditionally.

I am fully aware that not all stories end the way mine did. But if you're reading this and you had the abortion or experienced the pain of divorce, that doesn't disqualify you from experiencing the extravagant unconditional love of God to redeem your life, your dreams, and your future.

When Robert was about three years old, Bob and I were at my parents' house for dinner. Also there were Don and Mary Colbert, ministry guests who had come to our city to appear on my parents' TV show. After sharing great food and fun, I suddenly felt the need to ask them to pray for me. They agreed, and before doing so, they checked my emotions through muscle testing. (Each of our organs is attached to an emotion, and our body reveals areas of weakness.) The testing showed that acute grief was trapped in my lungs. Without knowing the story of our marriage crisis three years before, they asked me if I knew what loss or death may have attributed to such intense grief and regret. I proceeded to fill them in on the events and painful emotions that filled our last few years.

With a gentle smile, Don asked, "Do you want to be free?"

I said yes. I would have said yes a million times if I knew it would help. Everything about that moment secured the feeling of hope. Don and Mary didn't seem to have even a smidgen of doubt that this would end well.

In the company of my mom and dad, my close friends

Stephen and Pam, and Bob, what happened next was nothing short of a miracle. Don checked my belief system before we prayed, and then he asked me to repeat statements of truth—declarations. If my heart truly believed what I said, my arm would stay strong. This muscle testing was simple and accurate. I repeated after Don as I declared the following statements:

> *I believe it's a good thing to forgive myself.*
> *I believe it's good for Bob that I forgive myself.*
> *I believe it's necessary to forgive myself.*
> *I believe this is a good time to forgive myself.*

I was passing the test as I repeated these statements. Everything in my heart was in agreement with my words. That is, until they came to the final statement:

> *I believe I deserve to forgive myself.*

Forget it. No way. There was no way I deserved to forgive myself after what I did! My act of adultery had opposed everything I believed in, and it had sent everyone I loved into a state of excruciating pain. And as King David confessed in Psalm 51:4, that pain didn't compare to the damage done to my Jesus: "Against you, and you alone, have I sinned." I had hurt the very heart of God, my best friend, my confidante, my trusted Savior. In fact, if I could've taken "*that* Audrey" out of me, I would've pointed my finger in her face and told her I hated her. I hated what she did, I hated the pain she caused, and I hated the compromise that polluted her future.

With gentleness and compassion, Don said, "Jesus loves *that* Audrey. Jesus has forgiven her. And because you have Jesus living in your heart, you don't get what you deserve, you get what He deserves." I didn't necessarily feel deserving, but I chose to respond to this challenge from a heart of faith.

"Okay," I said. "Because I want to be in agreement with how Jesus feels, I believe that I deserve to forgive myself."

Now my heart was prepared to pray. Don asked me to use my memory to reach the buried pain in my heart, to remember the most painful moments of grief. I recalled the fear that paralyzed me the moment I learned I was pregnant, and how I'd fallen on my knees and lay on the floor for hours in the fetal position. Alone, scared for my life, with no hope for my future. I recalled the panic that overtook my children's faces as Bob and I told them about what had happened, and I remembered the countless nights I faced the wall with tears drenching my pillow as I tried to stay completely still so Bob wouldn't know I was awake. I felt imprisoned by my own selfish mistake, drowning in the newfound feeling of sheer worthlessness.

As I remembered, I allowed these buried emotions to rise to the surface. I whimpered, I cried, and then I let go and finally gave expression and ownership to what had been trapped for three years. I felt as if I was walking out of a prison cell, with each release of emotion being another step into a new land. As the fear, regret, and remorse received acknowledgment, I got closer and closer to a place of green grass, hope, freedom, and still waters. Jesus invited me to walk free, and I took His hand with faith abandoned to Him and let myself receive His forgiveness in full.

That's when I saw myself as He sees me. I'll never forget this image. I saw myself wearing the most beautiful glistening white robe of righteousness, with all the exquisite details of a wedding dress exuding sheer brightness. Light surrounded me. Then I looked closer and saw that my robe was slippery. The oil of joy covered it, and I immediately knew its meaning.

Up until that day, whenever I had left the safety of my home, I'd opened myself to the public ridicule that attacked me as rumors about my affair circulated. Although nothing was said, I could hear people's judgment, and I could feel their accusing fingers pointing at me, saying, *Look. There's that girl who says she loves Jesus, and does* that. *She doesn't deserve to smile. Did you hear that she's back in ministry? The nerve. She's disqualified. I sure hope she's getting the punishment she deserves.* In a world invisible to everyone but me, people possessed big black Sharpie markers and I felt defined by the Xs that covered my soul.

But now my robe was slippery. In that moment, in my parents' home, on that night that changed my life, every one of those painful Xs fell to the ground and disappeared. There was no space for them on my beautiful robe of righteousness. Jesus had paid the price when He died for my sins. He bore my mistakes, my failures, and my pitiful selfishness. He was perfect and became my righteousness. My righteousness didn't atone me; He did. In fact, my efforts to be righteous in my own strength were like wearing a filthy rag. On that glorious night, I received the gift that had been mine all along because of what Jesus did for me.

Imagine Jesus walking down the road, passing a person harboring secret sins. Even though He can see the bondage and pain that a life of sin displays, He never gives the person "that look." (You know the one: eyebrows lowered, lips pursed, glaring beady eyes as the head shakes slowly in dismay. *Tsk, tsk, tsk.*) No, Jesus always shows compassion. When someone is willing to ask, He sets forth a clear invitation: *Come, follow me, and I will show you the way and we can celebrate truth.* He gives the kind of life where you're not controlled or limited by people or circumstances. A life without secrets. A life free from sin. The kind of life that laughs in the face of the future. The kind of life where you wake up smiling.

That's the life He wants for you and me! Let's take this adventure together.

Fun Facts about Smiling

I have researched the science behind smiling, and it is a truly wonderful concept.* Once the smile-inducing muscles in our face contract, there is a positive feedback loop that goes back to the brain and reinforces a feeling of joy. It has even been said that smiling stimulates the brain's reward mechanisms even more than chocolate.

Smiling also seems to give the same happiness that exercising provides, in terms of how our brain responds. In other words, our brain feels good and tells us to smile, and we smile and tell our brain it feels good, and the cycle continues. In recent research, scientists concluded that smiling can be as stimulating as receiving up to $16,000 in cash. Wow. So smiling can change our brain through this powerful feedback loop. Our brain keeps track of our smiles, kind of like a smile scorecard. It knows how often we've smiled and which overall emotional state we are in.

Smiling reduces the stress that our body and mind feel, almost similar to getting a good night's sleep, according to recent studies. It also generates more positive emotions.

---

* Ron Gutman, "The Untapped Power of Smiling," *Forbes*, March 22, 2011, http://www.forbes.com/sites/ericsavitz/2011/03/22/the-untapped -power-of-smiling/#71ef0c7220d8.

That's why we often feel happier around children; they smile more, on average four hundred times a day. While happy people still smile forty to fifty times a day, the average person smiles about twenty times. No wonder Jesus promotes the concept of remaining childlike in our hearts (see Matthew 18:3–4; Mark 10:14–15).

Smiling has even more benefits. It breeds trust, makes us happier, and helps us live longer. And, most importantly, smiling can be learned—or relearned. Every child knows how to smile, but many people forget over time. (Hint: Smile with your mouth and your eyes. Have you ever told someone *not* to smile? That works almost every time.)

So what does it mean when we find it hard to smile? It's an indicator that we're carrying buried pain deep down in our heart. Jesus told us that He came to earth to heal broken hearts—my heart and yours. There are no exceptions; we all need our hearts healed, and we all need Jesus. When our heart is healed, we smile easily. We just can't help ourselves.

You may not be able to see it yet, but take my word for it: you have everything. In this crazy life and through these crazy times, it's Jesus who makes you sing. He's every line, He's every word—He's everything. He's a mystery, and He's every minute of your every day. You get to kiss Him just because you can, and your love for each other will see you through absolutely anything. He's every song, and you are singing along. (Thanks to Michael Bublé for the inspiration for some of that.)

Random Things That Make People Smile

* A loved one's voice on the phone from across the ocean

* People who are generous with tips

* The soft skin of a baby

* Friends having fun together

* Knowing that I do what I love for a living

* Happy parents in retirement

* Food that is meaty, savory, and creamy

* Seeing a favorite artist perform live and knowing the words to every song

* Sunshine on my shoulders

* Unexpected sweet text messages

* Good health

* Family and friends

* Music

* Leisure travel

* Knowing that every day at work I affect eternity

* Summer break for students and teachers

* Waking up next to someone I love

* Accomplishments of a loved one

* Funny TV commercials

* Cool summer nights

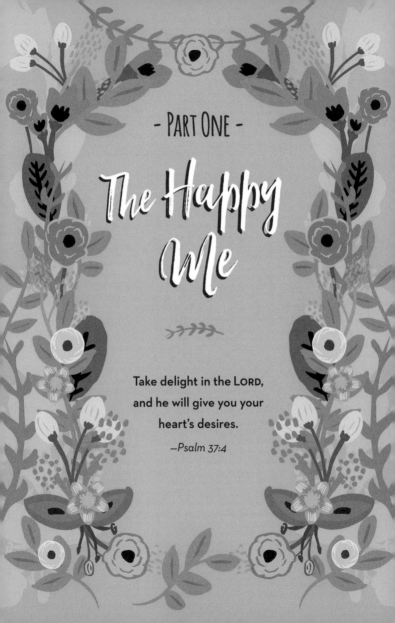

- PART ONE -

The Happy Me

Take delight in the LORD,
and he will give you your
heart's desires.

—*Psalm 37:4*

Day 1

Happy People

Happy people all have something in common. It's not that they're all rich, thin, successful, good-looking, or famous. Nor is it that they're the ones with the best toys, routine spa days, or the best bodies. They don't have the most popular ministry, the most Facebook likes, or the best-behaved children. Honestly, we don't need to have any of these things to be happy.

But there is one thing that almost all happy people have in common. Peace. Our culture tries hard to trick us, but let's join forces and unearth the treasure of true sustaining joy that can never be taken away. Whether we're old, young, rich, poor, short, tall, thin, heavy, successful, or average, to be happy, we need to have peace.

PEACE WITH GOD

Happy people are at peace with God. They have a divine sense of purpose, they know they are forgiven, and they have hope that things will always work out. They have a confidence in God that allows them to walk through circumstances that others would allow to steal their peace, joy, and happiness.

For years I felt like a disappointment to God, even though I considered Him my very best friend and confidante. When we feel like a disappointment to someone, we don't want to spend time with that person. But now I'm convinced that God loves me, and that no matter what transpires, I'm not a disappointment. I am at peace with Him.

Peace with Ourselves

Having peace with ourselves is being able to forgive ourselves for the mistakes we've made and letting go of the garment of shame. After I committed adultery, I beat myself up for a long time—judging myself, criticizing myself, and punishing myself for that stupid, selfish choice.

When Jesus asked me to agree with how *He* saw me, everything changed. He sees me as beautiful, forgiven, and righteous. I can smile knowing He paid the cost for this kind of radical acceptance, so I choose to forgive and love myself. Peace with ourselves is worth fighting for. No more pretending, no more performing.

Peace with Others

At times, people do and say inappropriate things to us. But because we are so loved by God, we're able to send away the offense and be at peace with others—even those who don't deserve it. Forgiving others doesn't condone what they did, but it removes their power to take away our peace. Will you let go of the offenses against you? Easier said than done, but oh, the joy for those who overcome.

Peace with Our Season in Life

Finally, happy people are at peace with their current season. Just as the earth endures seasons of freezing-cold winter and budding-growth spring, so do our lives. We encounter storms and unexpected torrents, as well as warm breezes and bright sunshine. We can't control or rush many aspects of life, but as happy people, we have peace with it, and recognize each season and lean into its purpose.

 Life Application

As you read this, you've looked into your own heart. You recognize where you haven't prioritized peace, and you can celebrate the places where you have. My husband, Bob, often says that peace is not the absence of fighting, the absence of problems, or the absence of challenges, but rather the presence of Someone. Embrace Jesus as your Prince of Peace.*

To wake up smiling is …

living every day with true peace.

---

* This chapter was inspired by a podcast by Andy Stanley of North Point Community Church. Our family has listened to the entire series, "What Makes You Happy," multiple times—so inspiring!

DAY 2
Peace Regained

"No wonder I'm not happy. I don't have any peace!"

Anything that undermines our peace ultimately undermines our happiness. If we explore a few of the things that rob us of peace, we'll see what makes us unhappy. We lose our peace when we're in disagreement with someone, and anger and frustration permeate our thought life. Or when we get competitive even though making unhealthy comparisons isn't appropriate. We lose our peace when we live with extreme regret and relive our stupid mistakes over and over again. Fear and anxiety are probably the greatest peace stealers, followed by bitterness, hatred, and frustration. This list could go on and on, and we all know the specific tendencies that result from our individual personalities and living situations.

I'm sure all of us can think of a circumstance or relationship in which we made a decision that undermined our relationship with God, our own heart, or someone else. We regret what happened. If we could go back and change things, we would, because we now carry around a regret that is chipping away at our happiness.

In Matthew 22:35–36, Jesus was faced with a profound question. An expert in religious law, hoping to stump Jesus with a trick question, asked which of the commandments is the most important. We generally don't think of commands having anything to do with happiness. In fact, we often believe that laws and commands get in the way of our happiness. Jesus answered, "'Love the Lord your God with all your heart and with all your soul and with all your strength and with all your mind'; and, 'Love your neighbor as yourself'" (Luke 10:27 NIV).

Loving God and letting Him love us are the most important things we can do. When we experience God's love every day, it combats everything that will rob us of peace. When we know we're loved, we're able to love others. The experience of God's love expels all fear, worry, and anxiety. When we value God's approval more than what people think, we don't compare ourselves to others but are at peace with our life and our season.

God has made us with a capacity for happiness. It is the core of who we are. God actually provides the way to happiness. To resist God is to resist happiness. I believe most of us would relate that a big part of our greatest regret is that it caused us to abandoned peace with ourselves, with God, with others, or with our season. What we did made us unhappy, and how we reacted afterward increased that unhappiness.

 ## Life Application

If you've been robbed of your peace, it's time to take inventory. Think about what or who has stolen your peace, then have a conversation with your heavenly Father and make peace. Ask Him to forgive you and cleanse you for your part in opening the door to bitterness, fear, or lies. The only thing the enemy has on you is his ability to lie and accuse. Call him on it!

Declare the truth:

I am not a disappointment to God.
I am forgiven and free from bitterness toward others.
I have no reason to fear the future.
I forgive myself for past mistakes.

Add to the list and make it personal. This is your new day of restoration. As peace is becoming your priority, you will feel lighter and will be opening the door so a new level of happiness can fill your heart.

To wake up smiling is ...
relishing God's forgiveness.

A Key to Happiness

Jesus said, "Blessed are the meek,
for they will inherit the earth." (Matthew 5:5 NIV)

Do you want to be happy? Embrace meekness. Before you say, "Wait, what?" let's explore the true meaning of meekness and remember that Jesus knew something about meekness that would give us the key to massive inheritance. Happy are the people who truly understand what it means to be meek, for they will have everything they desire in life.

To start, let's bust a myth. Meekness is *not* weakness. Jesus understood meekness as a powerful key—a proper estimation or value of one's self within the broader context of God's creation and love. Meek people face the reality of who they are. They know they are part of God's creation, that God is up to something in the world, and that they are part of it but not the center of it.

Meek people understand it's not about them. They're not constantly fighting for more followers, more friends, and more fans. They're not trying to be the center of attention.

Instead, they're willing to follow the example of John the Baptist, who said we can only receive what comes to us from heaven. In other words, they take advantage of every opportunity that comes their way. They do their best but don't strive to be something beyond what God has called or enabled them to be. They're willing to accept God's calling for their lives—no more and no less.

When we get trapped in measuring our success using this world's economy, we miss the benefits of being citizens of heaven. We can get caught up in forcing a certain result, and there's potential to miss out on what our heart truly wants.

For example, I want to use the gifts and resources God has given me to fight for families and help people love their marriages. But even deeper than that, I want to be a whole person who knows how to rest in my secret place and be still and know that He is God. I want my children to be confident that nobody, and no task or opportunity, takes higher priority than they do in my life. My heart truly wants intimacy with Jesus and a family who laughs together, knows peace, and gets to rest in unconditional love.

I know a Christian author who wrote an extremely popular best-selling book that reeled him into overnight success. Now twenty years later, he looks back and recognizes how the massive amount of money and fame has brought division and discord in his children, robbing his family of true peace and joy in his retirement years. He recently sat down with Bob and me and implored, "Don't ever let the *reward* take precedence over the *Rewarder*."

If our endeavors don't reach the success rate we hope they would, could it be that Jesus is protecting what our heart really wants? Is it possible we may get sidetracked by ambition and miss our deepest longings? Meekness is simply acknowledging God's wise assessment of ourselves, based on who He created us to be within the context of His broader creation. Meekness is being at peace, refusing to compare our life with the lives of others. Meekness is understanding that *striving* and *forcing* are like swear words in the kingdom of God.

 Life Application

Make the commitment to being confident in God's wise assessment of your life. With the Holy Spirit's leading, take advantage of every opportunity that comes your way. Do your best, but don't strive to be something beyond what God has called or enabled you to be. Accept God's calling for your life, no more and no less.

To wake up smiling is…

resting in being exactly who God made me to be.

DAY 4

Transferring Trust

Bob and I are citizens of both Canada and the United States. This privilege carries several benefits but also involves dealing with two different currencies, US and Canadian. All my Canadian friends and family who trade to US currency know the sadness that results when we give the bank a bunch of money and leave with a pretty poor exchange. It doesn't seem fair.

Let's explore some myths about currency. In the Sermon on the Mount, Jesus astounds us with His understanding of what it means to be poor. "Blessed are the poor in the spirit," he said, "for theirs is the kingdom of heaven" (Matthew 5:3 NIV). Rich people aren't happy people. Poor people aren't happy people. So then, who are the privileged ones who live in the kingdom of happy heavenly living here on earth? The poor in spirit—people who embrace their daily dependence on God, no matter what they have or don't have.

The moment we put our trust in riches instead of Him who richly provides, we are unhappy. The moment we transfer our trust from our heavenly Father to our earthly riches (such as our opportunities, our education, what we have, what we own, what we've borrowed for, what we drive, where we live), we become unhappy. Why? Because suddenly it's up to us to control outcomes.

And we can't control outcomes.

We can influence outcomes, but at the end of the day, none of us control them. And the moment we trust in riches, instead of Him who richly provides, we take upon ourselves a responsibility that is too big for us to carry. This is why we've met unhappy poor people, unhappy middle-class people, and unhappy rich people. Anybody who is feeling the burden of "it's all up to me" is, by definition, unhappy.

Jesus says that happy people are rich, middle class, and poor; they're happy not because of their financial status, but because they are poor in spirit and recognize that they're as dependent upon God for their provision as they've ever been. The poor in spirit don't attempt to find ultimate satisfaction in things because *things* are not an option. Our heavenly Father has invited us to live with that same idea and understanding. Ultimately, our confidence should not be in stuff; it should be in the one who provides the stuff.

If your trust in God were a currency of some kind, how much would you have? Do you trust that there's an unlimited supply in your heavenly bank account? When hopelessness wants to steal from you, do you simply withdraw from your account of trust and diminish the debt? Are you super rich when it comes to depending on God for everything? Treasure the currency of heaven that actually makes you happy.

Life Application

Declare your dependence on God for everything. Say aloud, "Papa God, I am totally dependent on you every minute of every day. I no longer want to believe that it's all up to me. I surrender to your ways and trust you like never before. Teach me to trust you. The more I get to know you and experience you, the more I trust you. So take me and teach me. I'm all yours."

Have a wonderful day, my rich friend!

To wake up smiling is …

**banking on trust
as our kingdom currency.**

Day 5

An Invitation to Happiness

Take a few moments and define *sin*. The broadest definition of the word is probably "something we know we shouldn't do, but we do it anyway." We all fall short of our own standards, so we could also define sin as "falling short of what we think is right."

Here's what we know is true of all sin: it separates. First, it separates us from others. Think of the last relational conflict you experienced. Someone sinned, either you, the other party, or both. You naturally conclude that it was the other person's fault, not yours. The other person did something you thought was wrong, so you retaliated, and the relationship is now strained. When sin is introduced into a relationship, the peace between you and the other person erodes, as does your happiness.

Second, sin separates us from God. The primary reason that sin separates us from God is that when we sin against someone, we have sinned against someone whom God loves.

If you mistreat one of my kids, you've mistreated me. I love my kids like a crazy mama bear, and God loves His children even more. We all know the beginning of John 3:16: "For God so loved the world ..." It doesn't say, "For God so loved the nice and good people"; it says that God loves *the world*, including the person we're in conflict with. So that sin has also crept into our relationship with God.

Let's take it one more step. Sin separates us from ourselves. When we carry a secret, we are in conflict with ourselves. We feel foolish. Sin separates by counterfeiting pleasure and comfort. It offers immediate gratification instead of ultimate joy and tells us it will take us further than we ever dreamed we would go. Sin makes a promise that it can't keep. It is not our friend, and it always ends in pain and ultimately undermines our happiness.

James 1:15 tells us, "These desires give birth to sinful actions. And when sin is allowed to grow, it gives birth to death." When sin is full grown (not a cute little baby sin that won't hurt anybody), it brings death. Every one of us has experienced this at some time or another. We invite a little baby sin into our life and justify it as no big deal. Then it becomes full-grown sin, resulting in the loss of a job, a relationship, or something else we value. Sin destroys.

The lie that has tripped me up in the past is that when I sin, I have to prove myself before I can step back into God's presence. But the story of the prodigal son is real. I have been that daughter—tattered, torn, and broken, running into the arms of my heavenly Daddy. He has covered me in

His love, holding me until my heart melted and healed. He has put a ring on my finger and called me His own.

It breaks my heart to watch people unintentionally undermine their own happiness and then spend a season trying to be happy when what they're doing will never make them happy. We're born with the capacity for happiness, and it is more under our control than we imagine.

 ## Life Application

Perhaps you're in the same place I was, thinking you need to prove your worth before you can present yourself before God again. Realize that you can't, just as I couldn't, and, even more importantly, you don't have to. You are God's beloved, not because of what you've done (or haven't done) but because of who He is: He is love. Run to Him.

He's awaiting your return, whispering, *Come home, my precious child. Come home.*

To wake up smiling is …

responding to the invitation to come home.

Day 6

Peace No Matter the Season

We all have favorite seasons. Some of us prefer the heat of summer while others love Christmas. Some dislike the rains of spring while others can't wait for the feel and smell of new life. Everyone has a preference, and there is no right or wrong. We experience other seasons as well—the seasons of life, some of which are sunny and some of which include storms that can potentially destroy everything we have taken time to build.

I have been through seasons of sorrow and seasons of bliss. I've had no job, and I've had the best job. I've had virtually no money, and I've had plenty of money. I've had no kids, and I now have had lots of kids. I've felt as if I had no church family, and I now have a great church family. I've had a disastrous marriage in crisis, and I've had a wonderful marriage (same guy). I've had times when I worried about my kids' hearts, and I've had times when my kids were in love with Jesus and making wise decisions. Hence the seasons of life.

Feelings and emotions go along with these seasons. I have experienced seasons of loneliness, despair, shame, regret, self-hatred, hopelessness, bitterness, and rejection. I've also experienced seasons of hope, peace, anticipation, safety, comfort, joy, and unconditional love. Then there are the seasons within my relationship with Jesus. Times of intimacy, times of distance, times of rain and nourishment, and times of desert and famine. Times when He's teaching me and leading me to new understanding, and times of being still in His presence and basking in His smile.

I've probably belabored the point, but I want to validate the fact that we are, right this minute, in a season. There are three kinds of seasons. The first is the factual season of life— where we live and what we're doing, how much money we have, what our family status is, and who we're living with. The second is our emotional season—how we're feeling and the level of hope we have for our future. And the third is our spiritual season—how we're experiencing God and His love for us.

Little correlation exists between these seasons, or at least much less than one would think. For example, we may have the most money we've ever had but still feel loneliness and despair. We may be living in near poverty but have the capacity for expectation of God's goodness. We can't try to adjust the season, but we can find peace within our season and determine to glean what we can learn from it.

When I feel desert dryness in my relationship with the Lord, it is then that I grow in my faith to continue walking the walk no matter what I feel. I learn to make declarations, and I feed myself with the Word of God even if I don't feel it landing in my heart. It is also when I feel the elation of hope in my season, when I refuse to fear the future and wonder when I'll find relief. I encourage you to do the same.

Life Application

Respond to what Jesus is offering in your season and be thankful. That's how you can step quickly into His presence and offer praise no matter what. Your circumstances and the people around you contribute to your life, but your only true source for absolutely everything is Jesus Himself.

When you get to heaven, you won't be able to offer Jesus the "sacrifice of praise," because when you're in paradise, it will no longer be a sacrifice. Offer up your praise and thankfulness in your season. Glean from Him, feed your heart with truth, and don't rush to escape.

> And now, just as you accepted Christ Jesus as your Lord, you must continue to follow him. Let your roots grow down into him, and let your lives be built on him. Then your faith will grow strong in the truth you were taught, and you will overflow with thankfulness. (Colossians 2:6-7)

To wake up smiling is …

noticing the gifts in every season.

DAY 7

Happy Like a Child

Luke 10:21 is probably one of my favorites. It reads, "At that time Jesus prayed this prayer: 'O Father, Lord of heaven and earth, thank you for hiding these things from those who think themselves wise and clever, and for revealing them to the childlike. Yes, Father, it pleased you to do it this way!'"

There's definitely a correlation between being childlike and waking up smiling, so let's look at the characteristics of a child. Some childlike traits are meant to be kept as gifts, while other traits disappear as we grow up and embrace adulthood. The trick is to identify which ones we should retain, since Jesus said that God reveals His secrets to the childlike. Consider these characteristics that we associate with children.

CHILDREN ARE INNOCENT

Harmful people, images, experiences, and personal compromises rob us of our innocence. One of the most beautiful gifts the Lord has ever given me was when He restored my innocence. I didn't deserve it. But He loved me, He held me, and He healed my broken heart. Did I mention I didn't deserve it? That's what makes restoration such a precious gift. I will be grateful forever. Because of Jesus, not only am I forgiven, cleansed, and healed, but my innocence glows:

> Commit everything you do to the Lord.
>   Trust him, and he will help you.
> He will make your innocence radiate like the dawn,
>   and the justice of your cause will shine like the
>   noonday sun.
> (Psalm 37:5–6)

Children Gladly Open Presents

Have you ever handed a child a present? He won't be likely to look at it and say, "Oh, you shouldn't have." No, a child will tear it open and hug it, kiss it, love it, and say thank you.

When Jesus ascended to the right hand of the Father, He left an inheritance for us that encompasses everything. Security, wealth, provision, peace, joy, favor, strength, and vitality. Forgiveness of sin, beauty, wisdom, knowledge, and purity. So why are we living substandard to this heavenly reality? It's time to receive from our Father in heaven and actually open the valuable presents that are right in front of us.

> For it's by God's grace that you have been saved. You receive it through faith. It was not our plan or our effort. It is God's gift, pure and simple. You didn't earn it, not one of us did, so don't go around bragging that you must have done something amazing. For we are

the product of His hand, heaven's poetry etched on lives, created in the Anointed, Jesus, to accomplish the good works God arranged long ago. (Ephesians 2:8–10 VOICE)

Children Don't Carry Burdens

Think about when you were very young. If you grew up in a safe and loving home, chances are your first waking thoughts of the day made you smile. Every day was the best day—a happy, wide-eyed adventure. Simple things made you giggle, and being playful and silly was the most natural thing in the world. Your parents took care of everything because they didn't want you to carry the burdens that adults bear.

Likewise, God doesn't want His children (including the adult ones) to carry burdens either:

Then Jesus said, "Come to me, all of you who are weary and carry heavy burdens, and I will give you rest. Take my yoke upon you. Let me teach you, because I am humble and gentle at heart, and you will find rest for your souls. For my yoke is easy to bear, and the burden I give you is light." (Matthew 11:28–30)

Life Application

Can you recall being comforted as a child during a time of emotional distress? This experience is essential to humans' ability to bond with others. Perhaps this comfort wasn't your reality as a child and your circumstances now reflect that. Your transition had nothing to do with age; it happened when you experienced pain and fear that robbed you.

My sweet friend, I want you to know that God is your Father—your perfect, doting Father who loves you more than you can even imagine. He wants you to be His son or daughter, trusting in His provision with the innocence and joy of a child. As you pray, express your desire to have a childlike heart.

> "Unless you turn from your sins and become like little children, you will never get into the Kingdom of Heaven." (Matthew 18:3)

To wake up smiling is …

receiving the beautiful gift of being childlike.

DAY 8

Pain as a Gateway to Joy

God can use pictures in our imaginations and even pain to speak to our hearts. A while back, I stopped in the middle of the day and decided to take a break. I put on my headphones and sang along to some of my favorite music. But then I was rudely interrupted by painful memories. I saw myself wearing a black T-shirt with the words JUDGE AUDREY stamped across the front. This version of me had a scowl on her face, and I could feel the sting of reminders and the rage of accusations that revealed my buried pain:

* Repeated lack of discipline
* Replayed words said against me
* Lies I believed about my worth

It had happened again. I'd allowed thoughts into my heart that were representing the accuser, satan himself. I identified the fact that I had let Judge Audrey ease her way back in my life, hitting me with debilitating lies that were not in agreement with what Jesus says about me.

We presume that pain is an enemy to joy, but an honest look at my experiences and my research in Scripture has revealed otherwise. Pain has the potential to be the gateway to joy. God created pain to be an indicator, because He loves us and doesn't want us to bleed to death. Of course, we all hate pain, but could it be that it has a great purpose?

Pain is a map to bring us to the place where God wants to hold us. Before we go a step further, I don't believe that God purposefully causes pain in our lives; I believe it's our own choices and the choices of others in this sin-infested world that lead to pain. But if we choose to stop avoiding pain, the end result is passion for others and new revelations and realities of Jesus. Through pain, we are eventually launched into joy and dreams come true. This is why the psalmist said, "Weeping may last through the night, but joy comes with the morning" (Psalm 30:5).

Many of us carry buried pain—memories so horrific that they're stuffed as far away from our conscious mind as possible. As we begin to feel more and more safe with the Holy Spirit, He wants to rewrite those memories, heal our heart, and remove the hurt attached to those places of abuse and fear.

Back to Judge Audrey. Instead of avoiding the pain, I faced it head on. With boldness and authority, I looked at the accuser and said, "You're fired." I didn't want anything to do with the voice of the enemy in my thoughts and heart. Then I imagined myself wearing a T-shirt that says BEAU-TIFUL AUDREY, because that is how Jesus sees me. I am going to encourage myself in the Lord and His promises, and stop the self-accusation.

Since that day, it feels like I've reached a new level of joy and freedom. The enemy is constantly losing ground in my heart, and I couldn't be happier about it. Having peace with oneself is an ongoing journey. Facing pain can be the beginning of freedom and joy. There is a direct correlation! When we are numb to pain, we become numb to joy. When we give our pain a voice, we can experience joy like never before.

Have you been listening to the voice of accusation about your weaknesses, your failures, and your past? If so, visualize yourself wearing a T-shirt labeled JUDGE _____ (insert your name). This version of you is mean and debilitating. Now silence the voices inside your head and heart and watch that accuser disintegrate. You thrive in happiness when you become kind to yourself and speak the language of your own Best Friend (Jesus). You are God's treasure and His masterpiece, bought with a price. See yourself as He sees you.

To wake up smiling is …
silencing the voice of the accuser.

DAY 9

Keeping Joy amid Sorrow

Joy is our inheritance. As children of God, it is rightfully ours and is not subject to a certain personality type or behavior style. Our personal expression of joy, whether it's loud or quiet, is celebrated. Joy is our protection against self-judgment and taking ourselves so seriously. When we can laugh at ourselves, we open up to freedom from trying to impress anyone. And when we have joy, it releases creativity, strength, and energy.

As Bob and I have helped people fight for their marriages, we've noticed that breakthrough often takes place after the couple has experienced a long-overdue belly laugh. Shedding tears of laughter is the opposite of having a pit in the stomach, and laughter truly is medicine to our being. So if joy is such an expression of God's presence, why is it so challenging to keep joy in our hearts when others aren't happy around us? Because just as joy is contagious, a cranky or angry mood can zap our happiness in a heartbeat.

It's rare for a parent or spouse to be happier than his or her unhappy child or spouse. When our happiness is conditional to everyone in our home and family, each morning begins in a mystery. We wake up to find out if it's going to be a happy day or an unhappy day. It's difficult to be happy when there's a dark cloud hovering over our spouse, our child, or our loved ones. We hurt when we see them in pain, suffering, or stuck in a challenging season. Moods affect the atmosphere, and empathy makes us want to go to their place of sadness or anger with them.

Taking on the responsibility to fix and heal the people around us is carrying a burden we were never meant to bear. We're not the source for our kids, our spouse, or anyone else we love. Now this doesn't mean we should be happy-dancing in their face, making them feel like losers. That's not love. And even though we're not anyone's source, we can be a significant contributor, and with that responsibility, we can be kind, serve, respond in gentleness, and be sensitive to the grief around us. We shouldn't excuse it or enable a victim mentality, but we can listen for the Holy Spirit's voice as to the best way to love unconditionally.

Let's make a choice to line up with heaven and live in hope every day. The fact that our child or spouse is unhappy will pull at our ability to have persevering hope. Even though we can throw a lifeline below and offer others a way out, it's their choice whether they're going to take the lifeline. We can live with compassion and empathy, but we don't have to join them in their hopelessness.

We are missionaries to our families, and we can nurture the presence of God and the presence of hope wherever we go—but only if we're submitted in our spirit. In our own strength, we'll never have long-lasting hope. We can have temporary hope based on a happy circumstance, but it lasts only as long as the circumstances stay great (which won't happen since we live in a fallen world).

 Life Application

Are any of your loved ones living in a difficult season of life? If so, ask God for the grace to love them daily, making allowance for their faults but never enabling them to steal happiness from others. Nobody—absolutely nobody—has the right to take away your personal peace and joy unless you give them permission. Define your role in all of your relationships when it comes to contributing happiness to those around you and stick to it. Then ask Him for a strategy to have joy and hope in your own heart, even in the middle of a gloomy atmosphere.

Joy is yours.

To wake up smiling is …

**being convinced that nobody
can steal my joy.**

DAY 10

Monuments of Joy

Bob and I will never forget a mission trip to India when we visited orphanages in a remote part of the poverty-stricken country to share the love of Jesus. Upon our arrival, we were welcomed by hundreds of children lined up to greet us. They began singing a children's song I had written called "You're Special." I can't describe what it felt like to have these beautiful children looking into my eyes and singing my own song—to me. Their smiles were contagious, and tears rolled down my face. These children had so little (materially), and yet they were filled with joy.

Another moment that had a profound effect on me happened years before on June 2, 1984, during our wedding. As a song played, an undeniable unexpected demonstration of God's glory filled the sanctuary, unlike one I have experienced before or since. I rarely talk or write about it because it was a holy moment, and even the unbelievers who attended the wedding were faced with the reality that God is real. He was very tangible in that moment as He kissed us with His presence and sealed our union with a testament that could never be taken away.

Moments so special they seem to transcend time and space are monuments of joy in our life. We can close our eyes, go back to that memory, and feel the extreme love of Jesus allowing us to have such a rich and precious experience.

In writing this chapter, I looked up the word *monument*. Its origin comes from the Latin *moneo, monere*, which means "to remind, to advise, or to warn,"[*] suggesting that a monument allows us to see the past and helps us visualize what is to come in the future. In English, the word *monumental* is often used in reference to something of extraordinary size and power. Monuments have been created for thousands of years and are often the most durable and famous symbols of ancient civilizations.

In the same way, our monuments of joy are symbols. They represent God's presence throughout our life—the experiences we've had with Him that no one can ever take away from us. They are in our past, they will never be forgotten, and they hold a promise for the future.

Another children's song I wrote describes a concept especially dear to my heart with the line "One of His greatest presents is His presence." The most monumental moments in my lifetime have happened in my secret place. Seeing the world, being on a stage in front of thousands, sure those experiences may seem monumental in the light

---

* Wikipedia contributors, "Monument," *Wikipedia: The Free Encyclopedia*, https://en.wikipedia.org/w/index.php?title=Monument&oldid=727912417.

of this world, but they pale in comparison to hearing the voice of my heavenly Father communicating love, advice, direction, and approval to my heart. Being viewed by multiple thousands on television throughout my lifetime means nothing compared to feeling the presence of Jesus beside me while I'm alone, driving, walking, or singing my songs just for Him. Oh, to have a heavenly perspective that recognizes the invisible monuments that the masses will likely never stop to notice. My precious friend, you don't need riches, fame, or talent to experience extraordinary life.

 ## Life Application

Think about the monuments of joy that God has placed in your life. Maybe you were thinking about them as you read this, smiling as you remembered the times God has kissed your life. Or perhaps you can't think of a monument of joy that stands out in your memory. Even if that's the case, not to worry. Right here, right now—this can be a holy moment for you. The Holy Spirit is covering you with a blanket of His peace. If you'll acknowledge Him and thank Him, this can be a moment that you'll always remember.

To wake up smiling is …
treasuring God's presence.

Random Things That Make People Smile

* The sound of the ocean in a seashell

* Big bear hugs

* Burying my nose in fresh, unpicked flowers

* Happy, polite kids

* People who have passion for their craft

* Being in love

* Passionate kisses

* No road rage

* Sales at the mall

* Big paychecks

* Surprise bonuses

* Doing something special for someone else

* Helping those in need

* A perfect mix CD

* Seeing my dog in the window when I come home from work

* Waking up and realizing that I have another hour to sleep

* Dinner with friends and a great bottle of wine

* Birthday cupcakes

* A rainbow after a storm

* Clear blue skies

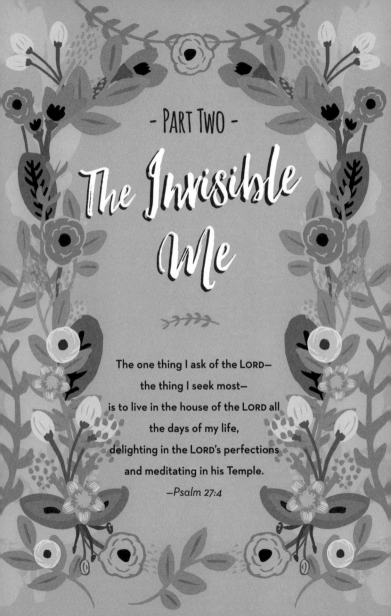

- Part Two -

The Invisible Me

The one thing I ask of the LORD—
the thing I seek most—
is to live in the house of the LORD all
the days of my life,
delighting in the LORD's perfections
and meditating in his Temple.

—Psalm 27:4

Day 11

Deepest Craving

Feeling close and connected to our Creator is the deepest craving of the heart, whether we're aware of it or not. What we look like, what we do for a job, who we're in relationship with, how much money we have … all of these things are deemed important by the world we live in, but each of us has been created by our heavenly Father. So heaven is our home, even though we're on earth for a little while. The closer we are to heaven, the more at home our Creator will feel in our heart.

> When I think of all this, I fall to my knees and pray to the Father, the Creator of everything in heaven and on earth. I pray that from his glorious, unlimited resources he will empower you with inner strength through his Spirit. Then Christ will make his home in your hearts as you trust in him. Your roots will grow down into God's love and keep you strong. And may you have the power to understand, as all God's people should, how wide, how long, how high, and how deep

his love is. May you experience the love of Christ, though it is too great to understand fully. Then you will be made complete with all the fullness of life and power that comes from God. (Ephesians 3:14–19)

Our deepest longings will not be fulfilled this side of heaven. Quiet desperation will lead us to something earthly (such as eating, shopping, social networking, or trying to be perfect), or we can recognize the thirst in our soul and be drawn to the source of living water and find hope in Him. Some of our deepest longings include feeling understood, supported, and secure, and experiencing adventure and true companionship. We get glimpses of these things on earth, but we won't feel ultimate satisfaction until we reach heaven. We weren't meant to be completely satisfied by what this world has to offer, because we will always long to be home with our Father.

Here on earth we often have to face and carry a lot. But don't think for a second we have to muster up enough joy and hope on our own. "Cursed are those who put their trust in mere humans, who rely on human strength and turn their hearts away from the LORD" (Jeremiah 17:5). When we try to survive on our own, we're turning our hearts from God—and oh, how we need Him for every moment of each day.

Coming home means letting Jesus into every part of our heart, welcoming Him to be at home there. Our heavenly Father has a message for us:

To the one I love and have chosen:

I'm so thankful for your tender heart. I see the real you. Your desire to be close to me and experience my presence is something rare and precious. You have lived so many years on a path with treacherous mountains to climb, valleys to endure. There's something about you. You have always taken time to stop and stare at the sky, embracing my beauty and worshiping the way I painted the skies. Just to let you know, when you notice, I can't help but smile.

I am giving you a gift. I'm going to help you better understand how you can live free from the cares and suffering of life, instead living the way I originally designed. Not just in theory, but truly full of hope and peace.

Living heaven on earth isn't just a sweet concept. I believe it's absolutely attainable. Through any circumstances, in any season of life, this can be us. It may take some time to align ourselves and begin receiving the full waterfall of His promises, but to start, we simply need to acknowledge our craving for His love and peace.

 Life Application

Pray this prayer with me:

Jesus, I invite you to make yourself at home in my heart. Thank you for loving me and covering me with the blanket of peace. I choose to hear your words that you love me and haven't forgotten me. I don't have to overthink the path of my life, because you have me where you want me for this moment, and I will walk away from self-judgment. This is my season to enjoy spacious places. In your name, amen.

To wake up smiling is …

accepting the truth that we long for heaven.

DAY 12

More than Meets the Eye

Waking up smiling requires us to wake up to the things of heaven—and they are invisible, which makes connecting to them intriguing ... or, shall we say, challenging. The mystery of life and the unseen is often avoided because of the unknown, so even believers become comfortable in soul talk and miss the benefits of living heaven on earth, where we can rest in deep confidence that the invisible world is actually more real than the ground beneath us.

In his letter to the Colossians, Paul wrote, "Since you have been raised to new life with Christ, set your sights on the realities of heaven, where Christ sits in the place of honor at God's right hand. Think about the things of heaven, not the things of earth. For you died to this life, and your real life is hidden with Christ in God" (3:1–3).

Deep down, most people are aware that there is Someone bigger and more powerful than themselves, the Creator of the universe. We as Jesus followers are invited to move through each day with grace and peace, but this isn't possible without being aware that we live from the place within us where God dwells—our spirit. There are many promises in God's Word—promises for peace, security, health, prosperity, and justice, to name a few—but for many of us, the truth of these promises is not always our daily experience. So how can we wake up smiling?

Positive thinking is never going to be enough. We have to acknowledge, grow, and develop our spirit man, and tap into the supernatural life we were created to live. Learning the art of "living from my secret place" (or living from the influence of the Holy Spirit) has been a lifelong quest for me, and in the last several months, God has helped me create visuals that have strengthened my understanding. These pictures give substance to my prayers when I start out my day aligning myself with God. I'm so thankful. This experience of visuals in my heart has been the main motivation behind this book. When we can "see" something, an invisible concept suddenly turns into evidence. What has been unseen is now visible.

Hebrews states, "Now faith brings our hopes into reality and becomes the foundation needed to acquire the things we long for. It is all the evidence required to prove what is still unseen" (11:1 TPT). Faith is simply the confidence that what we are hoping for is actually going to happen, the absolute conviction that there are realities we have never seen with our human eyes. When faith is alive in us, we are assured that the realities of heaven are our firm foundation, and when we prioritize the spiritual things and give significance to the realities of heaven, we begin to live a Spirit-led life. This is when we wake up to our true design.

 ## Life Application

Pray this prayer with me:

Father, I want to experience the reality of the eternal things I can't see with my earth-limited eyes. Open my spiritual eyes that I may see you more clearly. I choose, in this moment, to set my sights on the realities of heaven. I take great care in seeking you, and I know you take great joy in finding me. You respond quickly to me and snatch me away from the enemy's ploys. I have no fears. I am completely at peace. I look to you. I am never ashamed. Your light transforms my heart so I can smile. In Jesus' name, amen.

To wake up smiling is ...

being certain that our truest life is the one that is invisible.

DAY 13

All the Days of My Life

The psalmist David penned his desire for the Lord, and a divine existence, so clearly in Psalm 27:4: "The *one thing* I ask of the Lord, the thing I want the very most, more than anything in this whole world, is to live in the house of the Lord every single day of my life" (paraphrased). Obviously, to live on *earth* every day of our life is not an option but a requirement. But to live in *God's house* every day of this life *on earth*—that's an all-out invitation.

I want the same thing. I want both, to live fully on earth and fully in heaven. And if it wasn't possible to do so, David wouldn't have written that and God wouldn't have provided a way for it to be. I believe we are created 100 percent flesh and 100 percent spirit. Our flesh earthly body is living life here on this planet for a set amount of days, while our spirit heavenly body lives for eternity and is not limited by time and space.

Christ in us is our hope of glory (Colossians 1:27). Jesus

has chosen to make His dwelling place in us, and Colossians 3 says that our *real* life is hidden in God in Christ Jesus. We may have limitations as we live our days here on earth in this body, but we also have limitless opportunities to live in God's house (meaning in heaven on earth). So we are in Him, as He sits at the place of honor at the right hand of the Father, and He is in us.

Will you venture with me to wonder, truly wonder, if we are tapping into the fullness of life that we have been given in the Holy Spirit?

When God made humans, he formed a unique creation unlike any other in the universe. "Then the Lord God formed a man from the dust of the ground and breathed the breath of life into his nostrils, and the man became a living person" (Genesis 2:7). The very first experience Adam ever had of using his senses—his eyes, ears, and nose—was receiving the life-giving breath of God. He felt His breath, smelled His skin, and saw in His face the most beautiful eyes of love and validation that anyone could imagine in their finite mind.

Animals are physical beings, and even though they think, they don't ponder ideas and set goals. They have emotions (our Labradoodle, Winston, can express hundreds of words with the expression on his face), but they aren't eternal. Angels, on the other hand, are spiritual beings. They can reveal themselves as a physical being, but they are made of spirit and inhabit a world unlimited by time and space.

Adam was both. He was made from the dust, from earth,

so he was part of the earth. But God breathed life into his soul, so he became fully spirit. We are so much more than just flesh and blood. And God as our heavenly and very present Dad wants us to lean into the reality of our relationship with Him. We are not left alone to do life without Him; we are invited to live in His house all the days of our lives.

 ## Life Application

Take the flying leap into a deeper reality of living on earth *and* in heaven. Pray this prayer with me:

Father, just like David, I want to live in your house all the days of my life. I long for your presence in me and accept your invitation to live fully on earth and fully in heaven. Breathe your life into me so I know you as completely as Adam knew you, and lead me in my every step. In Jesus' name, amen.

To wake up smiling is …

**living on earth *and* in heaven—
at the same time.**

DAY 14

The Substance of Spirit

Heaven is just as real as earth. So my heavenly Dad is just as real as my earthly dad. I've started to give this whole idea a lot more attention in the last couple of months since I met Wendy Backlund. She came on the *My New Day* TV show as a guest, and Bob and I interviewed her. Let me quote from her book *Living from the Unseen: Reflections from a Transformed Life* so you can get a handle on how she has experienced this:

> Years ago, after reading John 20:19, God asked me if I know how He entered the room where the disciples were hiding. Based on the ghost movies I had seen in the past, I had concluded that He could walk through walls because He had no substance. In my understanding, dead people were ghost-like and not as real or influential as people or things in this realm. Then I heard Him say, "No, I have more substance than the

wall." The wall had less substance than He did; therefore He could pass through it. When you think about it, the created cannot have more substance than the Creator!*

This revelation helped Wendy place more faith in the unseen realm because she began seeing God and His realm as having greater weight than her circumstances and the things "seen" in the physical realm. The shift takes place when we begin to see the physical realm as what will pass away, and His Spirit and our spirit as having greater permanence and authority over the earth.

So, if our spirits are more substantial, more tangible, and more important than the things we experience here on earth, it's going to be a challenge to wrap our heads around this. That's when we ask for God's help to bring understanding. Romans 8:3–16 suddenly reads so much more clearly, knowing that the Spirit has substance:

> God did what the law could not do. He sent his own Son in a body like the bodies we sinners have. And in that body God declared an end to sin's control over us by giving his Son as a sacrifice for our sins. He did this so that the just requirement of the law would be fully satisfied for us, who no longer follow our sinful nature but instead follow the Spirit.
>
> Those who are dominated by the sinful nature

---

* Wendy Backlund, *Living from the Unseen: Reflections from a Transformed Life* (Redding, CA: Igniting Hope Ministries, 2012), 3.

think about sinful things, but those who are controlled by the Holy Spirit think about things that please the Spirit. So letting your sinful nature control your mind leads to death. But letting the Spirit control your mind leads to life and peace. For the sinful nature is always hostile to God. It never did obey God's laws, and it never will. That's why those who are still under the control of their sinful nature can never please God.

But you are not controlled by your sinful nature. You are controlled by the Spirit if you have the Spirit of God living in you. (And remember that those who do not have the Spirit of Christ living in them do not belong to him at all.) And Christ lives within you, so even though your body will die because of sin, the Spirit gives you life because you have been made right with God. The Spirit of God, who raised Jesus from the dead, lives in you. And just as God raised Christ Jesus from the dead, he will give life to your mortal bodies by this same Spirit living within you.

Therefore, dear brothers and sisters, you have no obligation to do what your sinful nature urges you to do. For if you live by its dictates, you will die. But if through the power of the Spirit you put to death the deeds of your sinful nature, you will live. For all who are led by the Spirit of God are children of God.

So you have not received a spirit that makes you fearful slaves. Instead, you received God's Spirit when he adopted you as his own children. Now we call him, "Abba, Father." For his Spirit joins with our spirit to affirm that we are God's children.

 *Life Application*

Read the Scriptures with a new depth of understanding that your spirit is stronger, weightier, and more substantial than your flesh or your sinful nature. With your natural eyes you see flesh, but with your spirit-trained eyes you can see through God's eyes and have His perspective. How incredible is that!

To wake up smiling is …

having faith that the unseen is more substantial than the visible world.

DAY 15

Understanding Spirit Substance

I was so challenged by the concept that spirit has more substance than flesh that I asked God to take me on a journey to help me understand this truth more deeply. I asked for a visual to make this idea relatable to me. Then I remembered something that happened to me several years ago.

I'd had a significant experience in my secret place (the spiritual realm). Jesus invited me to renovate a place in my heart, and the specific place was a ballroom. After a season of demolishing (identifying lies) over a period of several months, He helped me rebuild my belief system (establishing truth) regarding success and promotion. During this season, I faced huge disappointments and fear, which I was able to identify, and I began to put all my trust in God's promotion rather than how this world measures importance.

When the season was over, Jesus asked me to dance in love and safety. I no longer had to fear poverty or failure, which had been my strongholds. But amid this beautiful moment in my secret place with Jesus came a rude interruption. Two handsome men were watching me dance from the sidelines and distracted me. I could see their desire, and I was attracted to their sheer good looks. I turned away from them and back to Jesus, and then sighed with relief. My heart knew I had made the right choice; those two men were bad news. As soon as I looked away from them and stopped giving them attention, they disappeared. Whew! I asked the Holy Spirit, *Who were those men?* and He answered, *Fame and Fortune.*

Several months later, I was again dancing in my secret place with my Prince of Peace, Jesus, and I saw the two men on the sidelines watching me. As soon as I recognized the temptation to be drawn into their desire for me, the princess warrior in me, with new authority, was offended by their presence. How dare they try to tempt me! Instead of being distracted by them, I walked right up to them and kicked them with my high-heeled shoe. They instantly dissipated into dust. There was no substance to them; they had nothing. They were a façade, not even a little bit real. They had no power, and they were trying to tempt me with something they didn't even have.

From an earthly perspective, fame and fortune were tempting me to measure my value by how popular, rich, and influential I was in this world. They wanted me to compare myself to others in an unhealthy way, rather than be thankful and content. The voices of fame and fortune were torturing my thoughts and self-talk with degrading lies, accusing me of being a failure and not good enough. I had given them years of my attention, letting their teasing feel at home in my heart and in my thought life. I'd allowed them to rob me of peace in my heart. So, can you imagine how shocking it was that they actually had *nothing* to offer? I'm so glad I finally destroyed them with the truth of what God says about me.

Back to the present. Knowing that the Spirit has more substance than the things of this earthly experience, I brought this visual into my new revelation. The things of this earth are exactly like fame and fortune. Even though I'm in this world and my flesh has experiences through my senses, I am a citizen of heaven. I have new DNA, new blood flowing through my veins. My spirit is eternal, but this flesh is temporary. Fame and Fortune returned to dust in an instant, and that's how our earthly shells are compared to the substance of the eternal spirit we have been given. This helped me have the visual of how much substance the Spirit has.

 Life Application

Pray this prayer with me:

Father, give me eyes to see how temporary this life is. Help me to develop my spiritual senses so I won't have to live with fear of the future or fear of failure. Your perfect love expels all fear. Fear and love cannot coexist. And may I quickly recognize the distraction of this world, and all its pull toward waking up and looking at my phone and letting the news of the day determine my life. In order to wake up smiling, I am going to give you the first moments of my day. I want to experience your very personal love for me before I experience anything else. In Jesus' name, amen.

To wake up smiling is …

valuing the depth and substance of being a spirit being.

Aligned with Heaven and Led by the Spirit

Since I now understood that my spirit has more substance than my earthly existence, I decided to give my spirit a name so I could keep everything straight in my head. She is my spirit, so I named her Spirit Audrey. Spirit Audrey is completely surrendered to the Holy Spirit and is born of the Spirit; therefore she is already perfect.

> But you are a chosen people, set aside to be a royal order of priests, a holy nation, God's own; so that you may proclaim the wondrous acts of the One who called you out of inky darkness into shimmering light. Once you were not a people, but *now you are God's people*; once you had not received mercy, but now you have received it. Beloved, remember *you don't belong in this world.* You are resident aliens living in exile, so resist those desires of the flesh that battle against the soul. (1 Peter 2:9–11 VOICE, emphasis mine)

In my journey to waking up smiling, I had to give Spirit Audrey proper leadership of Earthly Audrey. I am Spirit Audrey living in an earth suit, and my flesh (earth suit) screams for attention. When my flesh is submitted to my spirit, my life aligns with heaven on earth. Jesus was the perfect example of having the Holy Spirit alive and reigning while living in an earth suit. He never let His carnal nature dominate. He had the same temptations we had, but He never gave in to them. He was 100 percent aligned with heaven.

When I'm spiritually aligned, I'm positioned to effectively receive God's very best. If I decree God's provision and blessing over my life, anything purposed against my provision and blessing can have no further say in the matter. My thoughts become aligned with His, my will is surrendered to His will, and I am in agreement with how He sees me. You see, He sees me as Spirit Audrey, already made perfect because of what Jesus did for me through His death, burial, and resurrection.

Now many people get weirded out when we talk about spirit and the spirit world, immediately thinking of ghosts and spooky-creepy stuff. What they're thinking about is the dark, evil side of the spirit world, which, of course, is quite real. But this side's power doesn't even remotely compare to the power of God, His angels, and the Holy Spirit He has given us. The enemy wants us to be full of fear when it comes to the spirit world so we won't connect to our wonderful and loving Creator.

Because spirit is invisible, sometimes we're tempted to believe it's just a figment of our imagination. We want physical proof of the spirit world, because "seeing is believing." Actually, the opposite is true for those who dare to live fully; life truly starts when we understand that "believing is seeing." The more we believe and experience the spirit world, the more we see what is invisible to the naked eye.

When Jesus left this physical world and his earth suit, He said that He had to go so He could leave us with a gift, which is the Holy Spirit, our helper and comforter:

> If you love Me, obey the commandments I have given you. I will ask the Father to send you another Helper, the Spirit of truth, who will remain constantly with you. The world does not recognize the Spirit of truth, because it does not know the Spirit and is unable to receive Him. But you do know the Spirit because He lives with you, and He will dwell in you. I will never abandon you like orphans; I will return to be with you. In a little while, the world will not see Me; but I will not vanish completely from your sight. Because I live, you will also live. At that time, you will know that I am in the Father, you are in Me, and I am in you. The one who loves Me will do the things I have commanded. My Father loves everyone who loves Me; and I will love you and reveal My heart, will, and nature to you. (John 14:15–21 TPT)

We can take comfort in knowing that we are not alone. If we've accepted Jesus as our Savior, the Holy Spirit lives within us. He is even more real than the skin that covers us. When we are aligned with heaven and led by the Spirit, we wake up smiling.

Life Application

Name your spirit Spirit _____ (your name in the blank), and give it leadership over Earthly _____ (your name in the blank). As you go about your day, keep in mind that your spirit and the spirit world have even more substance than what you see and feel all around you. How amazing is that! Ask the Father to help you see more clearly through the eyes of Spirit _____ so you are aligned with heaven and led by His Holy Spirit.

To wake up smiling is …

having faith that believing is seeing.

DAY 17

The Earthly Things Seem So Real

Several months back, I read about a man who memorized and then studied the same chapter of the Bible for five years. He started a neighborhood Bible study around this one chapter, which turned into a book, which then turned into an entire ministry. In order to be part of the Bible study group, members first had to memorize this one chapter. The man then described what happened after one year, and after two years. It seems the realities and depths of this message had the power to change his thought patterns, redirecting and changing his entire future. Doesn't that make you want to know what this one chapter in the Bible is all about? I sure did.

That's the tricky part. With intrigue, I grabbed my Bible and read the chapter. Sure, it was good, and I'd read it many times before. But I didn't exactly experience an epic moment where everything became new. The next day, I read it again and began to memorize it a little at a time. The best way for me to memorize is to create a movie in my mind that gives strong images to the words.

I started with verse 1 (the passage is Colossians 3):

"Since you have been raised to a new life with Christ, set your sights on the realities of heaven, where Christ sits in the place of honor at God's right hand."

Raised. I'd been taken up, taken higher. That was easy to do, to see myself being taken from where I was to a higher place. Even though I'd known Jesus all my life, I decided this was new. I needed new, I craved new, and I was going to take it by faith. I had been raised to this place, and it had a name: *new life in Christ.*

So I was actually going to this place where He was seated at the right hand of the Father, and I was going to live inside of Him. And the second I got there, I would get a new set of eyes, like a pair of bionic glasses, and these glasses would be set in one direction and one direction only. When I say *set,* I mean they couldn't be distracted by anything. Immovable. They had set their sights on the realities of heaven.

"Think about the things of heaven, not the things of earth" (verse 2).

I continued trying to create the details of this movie, but how was I supposed to think about just heaven? First of all, I've never actually been there, and the thoughts of earth are pretty much the obvious things to think about. Was this really instructing me to think only of heaven and not of earth? That was a pretty tall order. I had a lot of learning to do and had to ask God what it meant to think about heaven. I also had to stop making earthly things so important.

This is where people think we're nuts. "She's so heavenly minded that she's no earthly good," they say. That was my thinking too—until I heard the Lord's heart. He wants us to be so firmly established in our identity of heaven and the provisions of our heavenly Dad, so captivated by His extravagant love, so washed in His forgiveness, so free from the temptation to compare and measure success, so convinced of our own beauty and strength in Him, that "earth stuff" becomes simple, effortless, and, well, just full of pleasure like we've never experienced before.

It's hard to put into words what happened when I asked God about heaven. I started noticing colors like never before, and I started seeing details in nature that made me start crying. All of a sudden a simple walk with my dog turned into glorious worship. The more I thought about heaven, the less I thought about impressing people and the more I started loving people. The more I thought about heaven, the less I thought about what scared me about the future and the more I started laughing at the unknown and thriving in uncertainty. The more I thought about heaven, the easier and more fruitful life on earth became.

Colossians 3 became my heart and my meditation. Even after I had been reading it for a couple of months, the richness and the depth seemed to come in layers as it became the words I quoted before falling asleep and the first thoughts I recited when I woke up. What happened to me is really the heart behind this book, or at least a big part of it.

 *Life Application*

Start memorizing the first part of Colossians 3, and make your own movie, full of details. This is personal. You're the only one who will see the details.

> Since you have been raised to new life with Christ, set your sights on the realities of heaven, where Christ sits in the place of honor at God's right hand. Think about the things of heaven, not the things of earth. For you died to this life, and your real life is hidden with Christ in God. And when Christ, who is your life, is revealed to the whole world, you will share in all his glory. (Colossians 3:1–4)

To wake up smiling is …

**thinking about
the things of heaven.**

DAY 18

The Things That Lurk

While we remain here on earth, we will continue to wake up every morning, and sometimes it'll be pretty challenging to smile. Even when we know the truth of how loved we are as God's children, even when we are meditating on great promises, even when we are living a life of worship and experiencing God on a daily basis. Why? Because it's always a choice, and sometimes it's a full-on fight.

Hopelessness is probably one of the most discouraging enemies I face. None of us are immune to bad news, financial blues, relationship issues, and tired bodies. It happened to me this morning. I woke up and instantly thought of pressures and deadlines. I tried to redirect my thoughts to something good. It was early, so I didn't want to get out of bed and wake the whole house. Besides, things don't go well when I use a strong will to conquer the day. I needed to submit my will to Jesus and do life *with* him, not just *about* Him or *ahead* of Him. I needed perspective.

So I started listening to a podcast. *That should do it,* I thought. But it didn't, and it was a good podcast too. Then I simply asked God for wisdom and just listened. Colossians 3 came to the forefront of my mind. The truth in this chapter had been growing in my heart for so long that I went right to my "memorizing movie," where I'd created the images of what the passage meant to me. As I had countless times before, I spoke the words of the chapter.

Sure, they were just words, but no, they *weren't* just words. They were a sword. The Word of God cut through the discouragement and dissipated it. I received heavenly perspective and eventually got out of bed. The Lord led my day, giving me encouragement. I set my sights on the realities of heaven, and He lovingly led my thoughts and my steps. I might not have woken up smiling, but it didn't take long before I was.

Let's look a little further into Colossians 3, to verse 5:

"So put to death the sinful, earthly things lurking within you."

This Scripture doesn't say put to death every sinful, *evil* thing but every sinful, *earthly* thing. In my memorizing movie, I went ahead and imagined a coffin. I was going to put sinful, earthly things that had been lurking inside me in the coffin. (The word *lurking* reminded me of green Grinch-like smoldering molten lava that poisons everything it touches. To think that sin and earthly things look like that!) Worry, selfish ambition, greed, unhealthy comparison, gossip, slander, and all the things the world wants us to idolize—they all went in the coffin.

To put something to death, we change the way we think.

It's so simple, and I find that doing it aloud makes it more final. I'll give you an example. I put to death greediness, or worshiping the things of this world, in my heart. Put to death. Done. *Thank you, Jesus, for forgiving me, cleansing me, and changing the way I think. I choose generosity, and I choose to declare God's provision.* All we have to do is speak the words and truly want heart-level change, and we can put to death the things that lurk.

 Life Application

Maybe you're wondering what sinful, earthly things are lurking in your life. It's easy to identify them. What do you think about? The things that are robbing your thought life are the ones that are lurking. Take inventory of any earthly thing that is permeating your thoughts and put it to death. What an incredible adventure it is to put to death the sinful, earthly things that are lurking inside of us. This is our action step to thinking about heavenly things and not thinking of earthly things.

To wake up smiling is …

putting to death the earthly, sinful things that lurk.

DAY 19
What Do I Look Like?

True beauty and strength far transcend what we see here on earth. Our world minimizes the word *beauty* by making it superficial. Getting a visual of our spirit being offers substance to something that usually remains a concept or an idea. The Bible indicates that we will be able to recognize each other in heaven (1 Corinthians 3:12), so that confirms that our spirits know each others' spirits even here on earth, and our earthly bodies are just a copy of what we look like. (What a pleasure it will be to be reunited with our loved ones and worship God with them for all eternity!)

You and I look different, but because we are brothers and sisters birthed from the Spirit of God, we have a resemblance. Spirit Audrey (and I happily presume you are inserting your name every time I use my own) has already received her full inheritance. I will not let fear, shame, or unbelief rob me of believing the truth of God's promises. I am beautiful, without spot or wrinkle. I am always dressed in white, with sparkly diamonds in a crown or throughout my hair. My scepter of authority is part of my nature, and the purity of my smile lights up the world. I am always honest, and fully and completely surrendered to the Holy Spirit. My beauty is admired by kings and princesses. (I know that the guys will have a different interpretation of what perfect looks like, so I'll leave that one alone.)

Being completely forgiven means there is no residue of regret or self-hatred to add stain or blemish. Because Spirit Audrey doesn't carry the unnecessary weight of anger, bitterness, and resentment, I am the color of light. There is no darkness in me. I always have bountiful energy and fuel from the joy of the Lord. In fact, the oil of joy saturates me, making me shine with contagious sunshine as I effortlessly live in harmony with others (see Psalm 133).

Spirit Audrey is so successful she is literally part of my DNA. There is nothing I can do to cause God's purposes to fail, even if I try! The plans of mortals are many, and Earthly Audrey makes poor choices at times and gets distracted by worldly measurements of success, but Spirit Audrey does not. (You're still inserting your own name here, right?)

I am at peace with the happenings of the world, the "promotions" and the "demotions," and there is nothing that can rattle me or rob me of the confidence I have in God's purpose for my life. I am already completely approved and admired by my Bridegroom. I can take time to rest, knowing that my life has already been established. I will automatically know at every moment whether I am to take a step or to stop and rest. Sometimes I'm a child, and sometimes I'm a warrior princess. I never fear failure, and I definitely don't fear the future. I laugh at the unknown and thrive in uncertainty. God's heavenly poetry is etched on my heart.

In Jesus Christ, our spirit is not limited to the knowledge that can be contained in one human mind. We are submitted completely to the Holy Spirit, and His thoughts are higher than our thoughts, so we have chosen His thoughts. They are always established in the truth, and are never hopeless or doomed. Our ability to tap into Christ's mind gives us unlimited access to needed knowledge and understanding—divine understanding, revelation knowledge, and living understanding. Our thoughts are always pure, lovely, right, praiseworthy, and virtuous, and the peace of God guards our heart and mind in Christ Jesus. Creativity is our very nature, and our thoughts are new, exciting, and adventurous.

Life Application

Resistance will rise up when you read this chapter over and over again for yourself, applying your own name and believing it in your heart. Memories of when you have failed will scream for you to stop saying such beautiful things about yourself. Beliefs about your failures and weaknesses will try to prevent you from reading the words aloud. The accuser will tell you that you're being foolish and prideful, boasting about something that has never been proven.

As powerful as the resistance is, it's an indicator of how powerful this truth is to transform your heart and life. The truth that offends you the most is likely the very truth that will set you free. Push through, my beautiful friend. I know this seems way too good to be true, but you are God's child. Every child born is a reflection of his or her parents and their characteristics. Your Father in heaven can be seen in you, so step into the realities of heaven.

To wake up smiling is …

believing I am already perfect in Jesus.

Day 20

Spiritual Eyes

Our spirit being has eyes that can see things as God sees them. Spiritual eyesight is a gift from the Holy Spirit, one that can be developed as we take steps of faith and open this valuable present. Jesus told His disciples, "But blessed are your eyes, because they see; and your ears, because they hear. I tell you the truth, many prophets and righteous people longed to see what you see, but they didn't see it. And they longed to hear what you hear, but they didn't hear it" (Matthew 13:16–17).

Years ago, I spoke at a women's event in Canada, visiting a church for the second time. A sixteen-year-old girl remembered me from the year before and told me, "Audrey, I have been counting down the days until I would see you for the last 183 days. Every day I wake up in anticipation knowing that I am one day closer to my healing, because I know that God is going use *you* to get me totally free from my regret and shame." She then handed me a several-page letter detailing the sin of premarital sex that kept her paralyzed with shame and her frustration with lustful thoughts.

By the last day of the weekend conference, my poor, sweet, heartbroken little sister was mortified. Bob and I were about to fly home, and she was left feeling forlorn and forgotten with no sign of healing for her broken heart. I was tired from ministering, and she sat waiting for at least an hour for me, hoping I would pray for her one last time. I thought to myself as I approached her, *Jesus, I can't do this for her. She has to find you herself.* Half of me was desperate to help her while the other half was frustrated with the unrealistic expectations she put on me (mere human that I am).

We didn't have much time, and I became uncharacteristically direct, saying, "God is showing me that you are a very creative person, and that He wants to use your imagination to create a movie in your heart that you will never ever forget. Listen, honey, you need to close your eyes right now. Where are you? Tell me everything you see."

She described her surroundings, including a door.

"Perfect. Where is Jesus? Tell me how He's looking at you. Tell me what He's doing."

What happened next continues to confound me. God literally opened her spiritual eyes, and she could see. Here are some excerpts from her e-mail to me the following day:

First, I just want to say thank you for talking with me. It was so crazy this morning, those songs we sang, I could hardly sing them, and I could hardly keep my head up, I was so overwhelmed with shame. It was never that bad before. But here's the good stuff, 'cause the bad doesn't really deserve to be talked about anymore, or at least not without sharing the good ending!

After church, I was thinking about what we talked about, and I finally saw it! I saw how He sees me! I saw myself on the other side of that door in a white dress, and you know what Jesus did? I saw Him hold out His hand to me like a husband does at a wedding, and I took his hand and He pulled me into Him, and danced with me, and held me in his arms and sang to me just like in the song "We Dance." I finally can see that He sees me as pure, and innocent, and incredibly loved and beautiful! It's like I can finally choose to forgive myself!

On the other side of that door, it was like Jesus took out my heart … and took some of His heart and put it in me and threw the old one away. … I thought this was so cool because I always prayed that He would heal my heart and restore it. And He could've done that, but instead He gave me the very best—his best—not just restoring something and healing it and giving it back, but something totally brand-new, and something so much more valuable than just an earthly heart. He gave me His heart.

And with His heart in me, there's no way now that I will be able to forget His love because it's literally what's keeping me alive. … It's like I can finally breathe, and like everything is new like I never was able to breathe before. … And finally, when I think of a memory, it doesn't bother me anymore. It doesn't make me feel sick or anything! It's like it's so much further away rather than like

I'm reliving it. And I know it's just gonna keep getting better, and I'm gonna find myself forgiving myself more and more! Jesus is AMAZING!

Her faith made her well. Jesus met her in her place of desperation and anticipation, and He can do the same thing for all of us if we desire His healing.

 Life Application

Do you want to experience the movie Jesus has for you? The key is to ask God to soften your heart and then just let yourself go. Fall into His amazing grace and see through His eyes.

To wake up smiling is …

asking God to open my spiritual eyes so I can see.

Random Things That Make People Smile

* Home-cooked meals

* Chocolate anything

* Swedish massages

* Finishing a big project at work

* Kind people

* Sweet animals

* Random acts of kindness

* The perfect pair of jeans

* A good song coming on the radio

* New clothes

* A good night's rest

* Daydreaming

* A cat chasing its own tail

* The sound of children laughing

* Personal letters in the mail

* IMs (instant messages) that break up a bad day

* Jogging outside

* Meaningful conversations

* The sound of rain on the roof

* The salty smell of the ocean

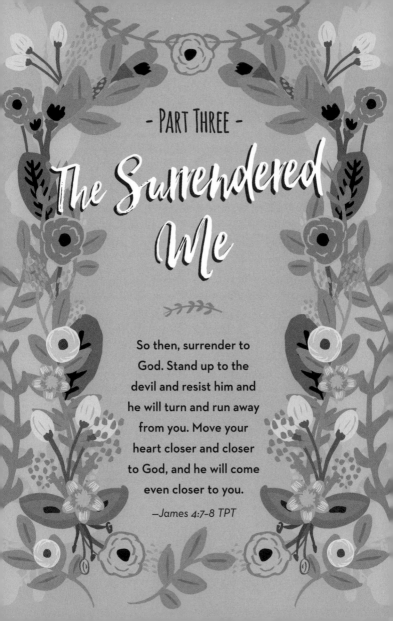

- PART THREE -

The Surrendered Me

So then, surrender to
God. Stand up to the
devil and resist him and
he will turn and run away
from you. Move your
heart closer and closer
to God, and he will come
even closer to you.

—James 4:7–8 TPT

DAY 21

My Happy Place

Isaiah prophesied over Jerusalem:

Your new name will be "The City of God's Delight,"
and "The Bride of God,"
for the Lord delights in you
and will claim you as his bride. (62:4)

To wake up smiling involves us doing things we have never done before. I'm not a golfer (or any kind of athlete for that matter), but I've heard the rumor that the best way to make a great drive is to take a moment and get into your happy place before you make your shot. To me, a happy place is an imaginary scene that paints a picture of paradise, pleasure, and peace.

Do you ever wonder why you crave a little paradise? Or why you make your best "shots" and best decisions from a place of peace? It's because we were created for pleasure and paradise—and they're found in God's presence and perfections. When I think of delighting in the Lord's perfections, I can't help but go straight to the original paradise: the garden of Eden.

In the garden, God was wrapped up in relationship with Adam and Eve. They would walk and talk about life in the coolness of the evening. And then came the sorrowful day when the enemy devised a plan to deceive Eve and then Adam. We call it "the fall" when God and humans were no longer woven together in harmonious union.

But with a heart to restore relationship with His people, God formed a plan of redemption that included more than sixty generations, including Noah, Abraham, and David, up to Jesus, who came to reunite humans to God and God back to humans. In the first book of the New Testament, Matthew begins the story of the epic reunion: "'The virgin will conceive and give birth to a son, and they will call him Immanuel' (which means 'God with us')" (1:23).

The name *Immanuel* encompasses the deep reality that God is with us. He is not just over us, around us, beneath us. No, He is *with* us. The Lord is completely inside our being like liquid love filling every cell in our body, every thought in our mind, every whim of emotion. Humans walked away from the paradise of being with God—they became separated—and then Jesus came with the very name that meant "I am now with you. Welcome back to paradise."

Since the beginning, our Creator God has wanted to be with His creation. Why? Because God, by nature, is stirred and moved by relationship. There is nothing apart from relationship. The Word was God, and He was with God in the beginning, before time and space. The Son was with the Father, and all of creation, including you and me, were the product of this beautiful relational framework of Father God, His Son, Jesus, and the Holy Spirit. Now we are invited into that framework.

Jesus was the embodiment of God, put into flesh. He is a living example of how we are to relate to God. We don't have to be a 100 percent-flesh person striving to act like God, be like God, think like God, and please God. We are invited to surrender to the Holy Spirit and be 100 percent spirit, connected to our very source, our unlimited perfection and delight. The more surrendered we are to our spirit—and His Spirit—the more paradise we experience. Our happy place does not have to be a figment of our imagination; it's real and it starts with surrender.

 Life Application

Pray this prayer with me: Father, forgive me where I've tried hard to do life *for* you. I thought this was the only way to deserve you. And forgive me where I've done life *above* you. I got caught up in ideas and goals and didn't inquire about your opinion or thoughts. I never want to think I am anything apart from you. And now, my precious Jesus, I acknowledge in this moment, and I firmly establish on earth and in the heavenlies: I want to do life *with* you. I invite you into every second of my life. The first step back to paradise is knowing we are together in this life. Amen.

To wake up smiling is ...

taking pleasure in doing life with Jesus.

DAY 22

Aligned for an Open Heaven

Paradise is sometimes described as an open heaven. It's like there's a window above us and nothing blocking us from receiving God's favor and blessing. As believers in Jesus and ambassadors of the kingdom of heaven, we have the authority to change the atmosphere with truth—creating an open heaven. Imagine all the blessings, promises, and pleasures of heaven funneling together and pouring onto earth like a waterfall. We want to be under that waterfall—not just watching others enjoy the bliss of the cool refreshing water soaking their being, satisfying every thirst, quenching every need. That rushing water is releasing uncontained laughter, unlocking dreams and the ensuing delightful relationship with God Himself.

This open heaven portal will follow us and expand our entire sphere of influence, splashing the people around us. We just have to align ourselves to be under it. This spiritual waterfall of God's goodness starts with surrender, and it's the great big exchange of His life for ours. It's living beyond what our natural minds can comprehend and stepping into the paradox of life that Jesus taught us:

> And whoever comes to me must follow in my steps and be willing to share my cross and experience it as his own, or he cannot be considered to be my disciple. All who seek to live apart from me will lose it all. But those who let go of their lives for my sake and surrender it all to me will discover true life! (Matthew 10:39 TPT)

Submission is our choice; it is a gift that we give to the Lord. Jesus never forces us or controls us, because that wouldn't be love. And God is Love. There is no fear or manipulation involved, just a beautiful, personal, handwritten invitation that says, *Good morning, my precious child. If you want to experience peace today, if you are up for an adventure of extravagant love today, I have some great ideas. I will plan your day with you, and yes of course there will be challenges, but we can do this together. I can give you everything, all the resources I have. My thoughts, my ideas, my opinions, you name it, I am offering my friendship, my leadership, and my strength.* Then comes our part—to submit, yield, and come under His authority and entrust ourselves to Him. It is a gift we give to Jesus out of our own free will.

I've followed Jesus my whole life, but I can't say I've surrendered to Him every day. I can also easily assess that the seasons where I did my own thing and followed my own plans and pleasures ended in disaster. If only I would recognize every time I'm doing this, but it's not always black and white.

In the last year, I've been saying yes to the invitation to wake up smiling almost every day. And something has shifted in me. I feel like I'm no longer an observer of this beautiful rushing waterfall of heavenly bliss. I have intentionally taken steps of faith toward Jesus like never before, and I'm feeling it. I'm experiencing heaven more and more each day. And—no big surprise—aligning myself under this open heaven started with surrender.

 Life Application

Choose to surrender it all. Tell Jesus in your own words that you are willing to share His cross and experience it as your own. Let go of your life for His sake, and then get your smile on. You're about to align yourself for an open heaven like never before.

To wake up smiling is …

surrendering my way to the waterfall of bliss.

Day 23

Who's Driving?

Living a life of surrender comes down to the simple question of, "Who's driving?" There are five people in your car:

1. Spirit _____ (imagination, intuition—perfectly aligned with the Holy Spirit)
2. Mind (thoughts, opinions, brain)
3. Emotions (feelings, moods)
4. Will (determination, motivation)
5. Body (appetites, cravings)

One of these five is in the driver's seat, another is riding shotgun, and the other three are in the backseat. The best way for this whole "wake up smiling" thing to work is if *Spirit* _____ is driving (the rest are dangerous drivers that will lead you to places you never wanted to go). That's all well and good in theory, but what if you have a super strong and active *mind* that wants to control of the wheel? Or maybe your *emotions* reign in most circumstances and get what they want. And what about your *will*? If it's strong, it will find ways to get to the driver's seat. Do we even want to think about what happens when the *body* takes over to get what it wants?

Now your mind, emotions, will, and body are all gifts, graciously given by your Father in heaven. But they work best as gifts when submitted and surrendered for perfect alignment. My daughter recently said, "My *emotions* are just extremely strong, Mom, and they want to drive my life. Just because of the way God made me, I'm pretty sure my emotions will always be in the front seat, but I need to keep them on the passenger side." What insight! I would confess that my *will* is usually fighting for driver's privileges, but what a revelation to see that it's best kept smiling by riding shotgun.

On any given day, any one of these parts can fight for control. About four o'clock on most afternoons, my *body* wants to get into the driver's seat, drive to the grocery store, and get some Oreo cookies—Double Stuf! And first thing in the morning, my *mind* wakes up on sonic speed, ready to determine how I'm going to conquer the day and which task I should take on first (on second thought, that may be that *will* of mine). All I know is that waking up like this doesn't necessarily bless Bob because he is a slower-to-wake-up snuggler-cuddler, and if I start sharing my thoughts and questions, I drive him crazy (I'm pretty sure the people around us love it when we are surrendered to the Spirit). When Spirit Audrey is driving, I can be at peace, calm my will, settle my mind, and be much better at relationships.

We need to decide who is going to be in our driver's seat. The choice to surrender our mind, will, body, and emotions to the Holy Spirit is one of the best decisions we'll ever make. Unfortunately, it's not a one-time deal. This is a daily confession, and one we'll never regret. After several months of doing this, we'll feel like we've tapped into yet another secret of alignment that is changing our entire approach to life.

 Life Application

Make this your morning declaration: *As I wake up, I immediately declare Spirit _____ the leader of my being—so righteous and forgiven, with the mind of Christ and perfect communication with the Father. I surrender my mind and thoughts, my will, my emotions, and my body to my spirit, which is then completely surrendered to the Holy Spirit.*

It makes so much sense why Jesus said He had to leave this earth so He could leave us with our Helper, the Holy Spirit. We were never meant to live a day without Him.

To wake up smiling is …

acknowledging that Spirit _____ is in the driver's seat.

DAY 24

Surrendering My Mind

Our son Robert is now five feet ten inches tall with a deep voice, but when he was a small child we quickly realized he had a strong intellect, an acute recollection of facts, and an incredible ability to convince and deliberate to get what he wanted. (I know, pray for us! That strong mind of his!)

Late one night after drifting off to sleep, I was awakened by him gently shaking my arm. "Mom … Mom … Mom, are you awake? Can I sleep in your bedroom?" (Now please know, Bob and I have never turned Robert away from sleeping in our room, so this scenario has played out about ten thousand times in the last fourteen years.)

Half asleep and with my voice groggy, I whispered, "Yes, of course, honey. Go to the couch. Night-night."

But it didn't stop there. "Mom … Mom … did you know that 89 percent of people sleep better when they're beside someone they love?"

Wow, Robert. Great fact. Don't care. Go to sleep. I'd said yes already and was pretending to still be asleep, so I didn't really wake up.

I share this story because it's sweet (they grow up too fast, and I'm so happy for my kids to want to be close to me!), but also because our mind is a gift from God—designed by God, and even more of a gift when we intentionally surrender it to the Holy Spirit. (Back into the passenger seat!)

Sometimes we idolize and worship a strong mind and intellect. However, what a revelation to understand that as we surrender our mind, we can anticipate divine understanding because we have the mind of Christ. So what's the roadblock—the resistance? Most likely pride and thinking we know best. I don't know if I would categorize myself as having a strong mind by any means, but I definitely admit to having an overactive one and arresting each thought captive to the obedience of Jesus Christ is no small feat. I also confess to having strong ideas and even fierce opinions at times, so this is where the practical part comes into play. I'm invited to surrender the beautiful mind God has given me to Spirit Audrey and then surrender my spirit to the Holy Spirit.

So how do we renew our thoughts? We are all meditating all the time, and it's not always good. Worrying, for instance, is meditating on the worst possible outcome. Condemning thoughts happen when we forget to believe that Jesus has really accepted and forgiven us. We can also meditate on punishing someone because we have been offended.

Having the mind of Christ results in having His thoughts, which are always in agreement with love and always full of the Holy Spirit's strategy for our life. That's heavenly alignment, and that, my friend, is when life becomes a beautiful balance of peace and joy, adventure and rest, understanding of our original design and the rhythms of grace.

 ## Life Application

Pray this prayer with me: *Father, thank you for the beautiful and strong mind you have given me. I submit my mind to my spirit, and then I submit my spirit to the Holy Spirit to take the lead in my life. Thank you that as I submit my mind to you, I am aligned with your mind, the mind of Christ. Awaken my mind and thoughts to be the gift that you intended them to be. Ignite new thoughts, witty inventions, and strategic plans. In Jesus' name, amen.*

Then, notice what drives your life when you're not living from Spirit _____ (thoughts, opinion, ideas, active mind). Identify which thoughts are debilitating lies you have believed or thoughts that aren't in agreement with God's love. Write them down. Next, purpose to write God's truth on your heart. This starts with effective biblical meditation. Find a Scripture (or a song or decree) that counteracts your wrong thought.

To wake up smiling is …
depending on God's thoughts.

DAY 25

Surrendering My Will

Years ago, in the place of prayer, I was feeling particularly close to the Lord—really experiencing His presence—and I asked Him, "What can I give to you?" It was my way of asking what makes Him the happiest or what kind of gift could one possibly offer to the King of all Kings.

Immediately, in my heart I saw a picture of a big present. A huge bow sat atop it, and its size and extravagance excited me. On the gift was written a single word: *Trust*. God whispered to my heart, "When you trust me, I can do anything."

Fast-forward to this last year. I love that my birthday is on March 4, because it actually sends a message: *March forth. Do it, girl! Don't just sit there. March ahead.* Something significant happened on my birthday. I was hiking on a mountain with Bob and all of our kids, and without planning, I veered off the beaten path and ended up alone for a few minutes. My thoughts were on Jesus and gratefulness, and I heard His whisper in my heart. *I know it's your birthday today, and I know you love to give me gifts. Your trust in me has been the greatest present.* He continued, *Now today is significant. I want you to give me another daily present. I want you to give me your will, every day, like a wrapped present.*

All of a sudden, wisdom and perspective from heaven started downloading into my thoughts and heart, like a waterfall. I have a strong will and am loaded with determination, but the Lord, in His love, helped me see my life from His (much higher) perspective. It's been permissible and fine to spend the first fifty years of my life taking on projects, setting goals, rocking my life, changing the world, and running crazy sometimes, but I was trying to do much more than what my Father was asking me to do. In short, a lot of the time I was just doing my own thing. And who knows, it may have been fueled by fear of failure, fear of lack, or fear of whatever.

My heavenly Dad gave me a present on my birthday. He said, *Audrey, Audrey, Audrey. You don't have to be so busy. I have an idea for you. Before you start your day, set some moments aside and tell me what your will is. Then give that to me, and I'll exchange it for what my will is for you. It's daily. And then you won't run out of resources. For the first fifty years you had an abundance of energy, zeal, and passion, but you're now going to tap into my wisdom and fine-tune your day so you aren't wasting any of your resources.*

"March Forth" last year began a new level of surrender for me. It started with me daily giving Jesus my will. Then it expanded to understanding the power of alignment. When I give Him my body, soul, and spirit, my will, my mind, my feelings, and my ideas, I'm agreeing with everything about Him, and taking up His cross and exchanging my life for His. Yes, it's a concept we've all heard about for a lifetime, but believe me, when I started doing this daily, like a relationally loving ritual, our friendship deepened and I started to wake up smiling more than ever before.

 ## Life Application

If you're like me, you're a determined person. So surrendering your will may be easier said than done sometimes. But you too can wrap up your will in a present before you even start your day. Include in this present your determination, your priorities, your strength, and your logic. Look up to the heavens and declare, "Lord Jesus, I give you my will!" Then, in exchange, He will give you His will—a beautiful gift filled with His promise to lead you moment by moment and a regulator for your strivings, so you don't overdo it—and the best motivator of all: joy in the journey.

Pray this prayer with me: *Father, thank you for courage, determination, and a strong will. I submit my will to my spirit, and then I submit my spirit to the Holy Spirit to take the lead in my life. Thank you that as I submit my will to you, I am aligned with your perfect will, your purposes, and your resources. Awaken my will to do exactly (and only) what I see you doing today. In Jesus' name, amen.*

To wake up smiling is ...
cherishing the opportunity to submit my will to God.

DAY 26

Surrendering My Emotions

Several comparisons in Proverbs 15:13–15 (TPT) disclose the powerful choices we have when it comes to emotions.

> A cheerful heart puts a smile on your face,
> but a broken heart leads to depression.
> Lovers of God hunger after truth,
> but those without understanding
> feast on foolishness and don't even realize it.
> Everything seems to go wrong
> when you feel weak and depressed.
> But when you choose to be cheerful,
> every day will bring you more and more joy
> and fullness.

If we think we're slaves to our emotions, we should think again. Instead of letting our external circumstances be our determining factor, we need to get ready to awaken our possibilities to agree with God.

In this lifestyle of waking up smiling, I have to purpose within my heart that my emotions are not in charge. They are submitted to Spirit Audrey, who is submitted to the Holy Spirit. The Holy Spirit emotions are love, joy, goodness, faith, self-control, patience, peace, gentleness, and meekness. We can't deny or rush seasons of grief and loss, but even in these places we can invite Jesus to heal our emotions.

Emotions are a strong driving force in life, from both a negative and positive standpoint. But surrendering our emotions to our spirit is a powerful intention on the path to changing everything about our world. It's not difficult to see the reality of earth and live like the world—anyone can do that—but can we see another possibility? We can harmonize our beliefs with what He says about us. We tend to think that "big" happens when we do something big externally, but the biggest things happen when we establish the beliefs of our heart.

The combination of information and emotion creates a belief. Like it or not, our emotions are God-given, and they can work for or against us. And we're going to use and need our emotions to experience God. Life gets stuck when we let our emotions take the driver's seat. Our emotions are the determining factor of whether we'll stay where we are or see life through the realities of heaven.

Are your emotions leading you, or are you leading your emotions? Faith is ignited when you choose Jesus and surrender your emotions whether you feel like it or not. Perhaps you simply haven't "felt" anything for a long time. Your emotions have been in the corner of the backseat. You feel numb—not sad or happy, just dull. You're not alone, and you're not broken.

Jesus is reaching out to you right now, asking you to let Him hold you. He will hold you and love you as your heavenly Father until you finally let go of your resistance and rest in His embrace. Close your eyes. Don't pressure yourself to "feel" anything, for these things can't be rushed. But do rest in the arms of your heavenly Father until you start to feel. Your first emotion will likely be sadness. Your barrier will break with tears. These are such important healing tears. My sweet friend, don't try to stop them.

 ## Life Application

Pray this prayer with me: *Father, thank you for the gift of emotions so I can feel joy, feel pain, and feel life. I submit my emotions to my spirit, and then I submit my spirit to the Holy Spirit to take the lead in my life. Thank you that as I submit my emotions to you, I am aligned with your emotions of joy, peace, patience, hopefulness, and bliss. Today is my day to look inside my heart and line up my emotions with the realities of heaven. I have a cheerful heart and a smile on my face. I hunger after the truth, and refuse to feast on foolishness for one more day. Even when things seem to go wrong and I feel weak and depressed, I will choose to be cheerful. My life is full of joy because God wants to miraculously provide peace, assurance, and reward. In Jesus' name, amen.*

To wake up smiling is …

**being dependent on
God's emotions as my own.**

Day 27

Surrendering My Stuff

When I was in elementary school, having a pack of gum was a rare treat. Even though it only cost a dime, those dimes were not always readily available, believe me. I grew up in a Holy Spirit-filled home where we lived by faith—and I say that quite literally. For years, my parents were missionaries to our city and didn't receive salaries. The crazy thing is, when I look back, I always thought I had extra. Not just enough but *extra*.

One summer during my childhood, a local grocery store burned down, and the manager, who knew my dad, said to him, "Hey, Willard. I'll bet some of this canned food is still fine. Before they come and clean up all the debris from the fire, do you want to bring a truck and check it out?" That was the beautiful summer day when manna came down from heaven. Our backyard became a big storage cabinet. "Come on, kids!" Dad said. "Let's sort out our loot. Open every box." The labels were burned off most of the cans, but that just added to the adventure. For months afterward, I'd hear, "Audrey, go downstairs and grab some cans for dinner."

We also ended up with several cases (cases!) of Big Red

chewing gum, so I was "that girl" at school who not only always had enough chewing gum but even had extra. It was easy to be generous with my gum.

A few years later, a bright yellow sunshiny dress was by far my favorite piece of clothing. Somebody had given it to my mom, and it didn't fit her, so it was given to me. I wore it on days when I wanted to feel extra special. Crazy to think how a piece of clothing can bring such joy.

Now my brother was three years older than I, so his friends were super cool, and I always felt honored to be with them. During one of our times together, one of the girls he hung out with asked if she could borrow my yellow dress for a party she would be attending. I didn't hesitate, amazed that I would have something that this cool girl wanted. I was over the moon, to be honest.

You can probably guess what happened. The yellow dress never came back. Whenever I mustered up the courage to ask her about it, she gave obscure excuses, and I just kept hoping she would return it one day.

My mom noticed my sadness about it, and after school one day she just held me and let me cry. "You know, Audrey, if you choose in your heart to *give* her that dress, then it won't feel like she stole it. And even better, you will receive the blessing from that seed of generosity."

So I took a breath and offered the sacrifice of generosity.

When it comes to stuff, let's just surrender it all to the Lord. We're just stewards anyway, and we can't take any of our material items to heaven with us. Then, let's take it to the next level, slap greed right in the face, and be generous. Bob and I have a saying: *If something is in question, always err on the side of generosity.*

As God is generous to us, so we must be generous to others.

 ## Life Application

Surrender your stuff to the Lord, and remember that you have extra. Maybe it's peace (you can't help but be chill) or faith (you're oozing with it) or compassion (you want to take care of everybody). Ask God what your unique "extra" is. For me, it's encouragement. My friends and family will vouch that I will come up with some kind of optimistic encouraging remark even when someone has no desire to hear it. But I've got extra, so I want to share it.

Receive this message from Jesus: *I will give you ideas of how you can be a giver today. Be ready to give words of encouragement to others, give a smile, give hope, or give something away. Just be generous and notice how your heart is opened up to receive joy. I want to give you more joy than you've ever had before. Just as an antique is lovingly restored, I have plans to restore the joy of your salvation. I'm that good, and there is nothing I will hold back from you.*

To wake up smiling is …
**soaking in the security that
I am always provided for.**

Day 28

Surrendering My Appetites

My daily prayer of alignment is declaring, "Spirit Audrey, take your place as the rightful leader of my being. Since you are submitted to the Holy Spirit, you are the best leader of my being, completely influenced by God. I surrender every part of my mind, soul, and body to you."

As soon as we start submitting to the influence of God, He begins to help us with our human appetites and longings—and that is good news for all of us! It means that when we surrender our bad habits and unhealthy choices, we come into agreement with Him. It also means we align ourselves with extreme health and limitless energy. Paul wrote, "Don't you realize that your body is the temple of the Holy Spirit, who lives in you and was given to you by God? You do not belong to yourself" (1 Corinthians 6:19).

Our bodies are the Holy Spirit's living room, a love gift from God. The body was intended to be a source of great wonder and awe, and all of our appetites have their source in God. They may be deeply misused in this world, but the Creator of the appetites is the Son of God Himself. That being the case, the use of our appetites should be encouraged, but they should be used profitably and not be allowed to become enslaving. Appetites are morally neutral as gifts of God; it is what we do with them that matters.

Every human appetite for food, sex, comfort, and pleasure can be suitably satisfied within the realm of healthy instructions from the Lord. If our body has authority, it will take over. If I let my body have whatever it craves, I would live on pancakes and take the occasional slow walk—and that would pretty much satisfy me. Some people would give in to pornography, substitutes for comfort and escape, addictions, and bad habits, just to name a few. But life goes better when we keep our bodies under wise instruction and surrender daily.

Have you ever tried to make a lifestyle change? Making a determined effort only lasts as long as we remain strong willed, and before long we're tired of trying so hard and revert to our old habits. If we're sick, tired, overweight, or just mad at ourselves, we need to realize that God is giving us an invitation to let His truth set us free. The Holy Spirit will help us identify the lies that have limited us and give us the emotional and spiritual capacity to overcome challenges.

When I think about surrendering my appetites, I also consider my health and the difference between real and false rest and energy. False energy is caffeine, sugar, simple carbohydrates, amphetamines, and cortisol; true energy is raw food, lean proteins, movement and exercise, stretching and strengthening, playing and laughing. False rest is alcohol, sleeping pills, overeating, television, and painkillers;

true rest (renewal and recovery) takes place through regular breaks, meditating, sleeping, vacations, immersing in nature, worship, massage, and unplugging from technology.

God created us to enjoy our life and our family, so we need to take care of our physical health as well as our spiritual health. And while there are no pat answers when it comes to being healthy in all of our appetites (because there are so many opinions, tweaks, and ideas), surrendering our body, mind, and spirit to the life of the Holy Spirit is a great place to begin.

 ## Life Application

Pray this prayer with me: *Father, I surrender my body and all my appetites, cravings, and desires to my spirit, which is submitted to the Holy Spirit. I love myself just as I am, and invite you to minister to my self-worth. Out of love, I will take care of my body with optimum fuel, real rest, and healthy food choices. I know that making changes that last requires writing truth on my heart, as well as building positive rituals and highly specific behaviors that become automatic over time and no longer require conscious intention. I am going to give room for Spirit _____ to influence my life. In Jesus' name, amen.*

To wake up smiling is …

learning true rest, energy, and self-control.

DAY 29

Surrendering My Opinions

Proverbs 13:1 (TPT) says, "A wise son or daughter desires a father's discipline, but the know-it-all never listens to correction." Have you ever met people who seem to know everything? No matter what you tell them, their answer is, "I know." Even when you get personal and tell them something that the Lord showed you, they quickly say, "Oh, I know. That's happened to me before. I know." And when something is in question, they don't have to question themselves because … (you get it) they know. They really know. And they are right.

My heart starts to race when I think about these people, because they drive me nuts—until I get heart-wrenchingly honest and come to terms with the fact that I is one. (Yes, I used that improper grammar on purpose—you see, I know that wasn't correct.) This morning I was reading Proverbs in *The Passion Translation* and one particular line stared me in the face and revealed my very soul: "A fool is in love with his own opinion, but wisdom means being teachable" (12:15).

There are so many things I am in love with. Sunshine. Jesus. My kids. Peace. My mom and dad. Smiling. Bob (especially Bob). But I really do *not* want to be in love with my own opinion. In fact, I want to learn to listen without wondering what I'm going to say next. I want to surrender my opinion to the Lord. I want God's opinion. And I want to be gentle and see other's opinions as a gift to me, offering opportunity to grow and learn and be rich in wisdom.

Two nights ago, we were on an errand to buy Robert a new pair of jeans, and he made sure that before we arrived at the store, I was in agreement with him that he was not going to try the jeans on in the dressing room. He hates doing that. I started talking about how he's growing, and how different brand names have a totally different fit, and the importance of trying them on. He wouldn't have it. He started trying to out-talk me and argue his point, hoping to get his own way. Here's how it went down:

Me: Robert, do you really think that you know more about jeans than I do?

Robert: Yes, Mom, I really do.

Me (laughing): You are such a teenager.

Robert: What's that supposed to mean?

Me: It means you think you know more than me about life, even though I have fifty years of experience!

Robert: Well, I do. I actually believe I do know more than you.

Case in point.

As I reiterated this to my mom this morning, we laughed together and she reminded me of a series of programs that Dutch Sheets taught on *My New Day* many years ago, about maturing in Christ. He talked about how many Christ followers stay in the teenager stage and actually think they know better than God when it comes to certain situations or people. "Mom," I said, "I go so far, knowing how much I rely on my Father and acknowledging how His ways are higher than mine, and His thoughts are higher than mine … but then I have to catch myself."

It's easy to rely on our own minds, intellect, and limited experience when it comes to life, especially when we tend to fall in love with our own opinions. But in the end, it's God's opinions that truly matter.

Pray this prayer with me: *Father, I surrender my opinion to my spirit, which is submitted to the Holy Spirit. Today is my day to hear your opinion for the decisions I make, the places I go, and the thoughts I think. I am in love with you, and you discipline me because you love me so much. I desire your ideas, your ways, and your thoughts. Today is my day to thank you for confiding in me and commanding me to love others. By your grace and wisdom, I will do that well today—in your way, remembering that I am your chosen child. Jesus, I love waking up with you. I love feeling close and connected to you. I trust you and I love you. Amen.*

To wake up smiling is …
being in love with God's opinion.

DAY 30

Surrendering My Idea of Success

I clearly remember the day I opened my journal to vent a little. I was exhausted from trying to be "amazing" and working hard to fulfill everything I thought I was supposed to do. I poured myself a cup of hot tea as I poured out my complaints to Jesus. I felt like a disappointment—a failure—and I couldn't think of anything I could do to be more successful.

At that moment I closed my eyes, and in my imagination I saw a mountain. It was the mountain of success, and I was climbing it hard, forcing myself to persevere and push back disappointment, temptation to complain, and exhaustion. I looked up and saw people who had climbed much higher than I. *How did they get to be that successful?* I asked myself as twangs of jealousy shot through my heart. Then I looked below me and felt comforted by seeing people below me who struggled to get to where I was. *Well, at least I'm doing better than them.*

Fortunately, I recognized the ridiculous and selfish thoughts that polluted my heart. I hated that mountain. I hated what it did to my heart, and I was exhausted from trying so hard. Enter Jesus. He simply reminded me of one of my favorite Psalms: "He who dwells in the secret place of the Most High shall abide under the shadow of the Almighty" (91:1 NKJV). (Don't you just love how He brings us wisdom and perspective with such love and patience?)

Two words jumped out like never before. *Most High.* I am invited by the King of Kings to dwell in His secret place and abide in His presence and live life from His dwelling. And guess what? It's higher than any stupid mountain of success, it's safer, and there's no room for comparison. On that day, I chose to embrace the truth and immediately experienced His peace, His presence, and His abiding liquid love. Oh, sweet Jesus. Then, of course, I took a big stick of holy dynamite and blew up the mountain. I had (and have) no desire to ever climb it again. And why should I? I am chosen by God to be His precious, beautiful, and beloved daughter. Secure in His love, I have no need to compare myself to anyone.

> Blessed are you who give yourselves over to GOD,
> turn your backs on the world's "sure thing,"
> ignore what the world worships;
> The world's a huge stockpile
> of GOD-wonders and God-thoughts.
> Nothing and no one
> comes close to you!
> I start talking about you, telling what I know,
> and quickly run out of words.
> Neither numbers nor words account for you.

Doing something for you, bringing something to you—
that's not what you're after.
Being religious, acting pious—
that's not what you're asking for.
You've opened my ears so I can listen.
So I answered, "I'm coming.
I read in your letter what you wrote about me,
And I'm coming to the party you're throwing for me."
That's when God's Word entered my life,
became part of my very being. (Psalm 40:4–8 MSG)

 ## Life Application

Today is your day to ponder these questions: Am I climb-ing the mountain of success? Am I deriving my identity from how successful people perceive me to be? If so, it's time to change your dwelling place. Blow up the mountain and choose to live in the secret place of the Most High. Under the shadow of His wings you are safe, you are at rest, and you will effortlessly fulfill your purpose.

Surrender your idea of success and happily embrace the security you have in your Father's love. My friend, it's a great day to blow up mountains.

To wake up smiling is …

**being aware that I already dwell
in the highest place.**

Random Things That Make People Smile

* People with big smiles

* A witty book or restaurant review

* Kids being kids without a worry in the world

* Flipping eggs without breaking the yolk

* A great cup of coffee

* When my home is filled with people I love

* The innocent wonder of a child enjoying the world

* Family holidays

* Thinking about somebody, having my phone ring, and seeing the caller is the person I was just thinking about

* An elderly couple holding hands, still in love

* Tracking a package and seeing "out for delivery"

* Making someone smile or laugh

* Finding money in my pockets

* Dessert

* People smiling at me simply to be kind

* Playing board games

* A puppet show

* Coming home after a long trip

* People who serve "the least of these"

- PART FOUR -

The Hope-Filled Me

Give all your worries
and cares to God,
for He cares about you.

–1 Peter 5:7

DAY 31

A Recipe for Hope

Let me tell you what happens when we have hope. We laugh easily, we wake up smiling, and we're protected by the supershield of Holy Spirit perspective. In the deepest part of us, we no longer have buttons and triggers, because we've dealt with buried pain, the Spirit is driving, and our will, emotions, mind, and body are blessed and awesome but not in charge.

Feeding our spirit is not just a good idea; it's a recipe for hope. The Spirit-led life is our ticket to wholeness (peace and joy) and protection from the influences of this world (greed, fear, pride) snatching us away. We are not slaves to despair, dear friend, so this is our day to walk free. The power is in a choice, and as cliché as that may sound, it's real.

And his fullness fills you, even though you were once like corpses, dead in your sins and offenses. It wasn't that long ago that you lived in the religion, customs, and values of this world, obeying the dark ruler of the earthly realm who fills the atmosphere with his authority, and works diligently in the hearts of those who are disobedient to the truth of God. The corruption that was in us from birth was expressed through the deeds and desires of our self-life. We lived by whatever our natural cravings and thoughts our minds dictated, living as rebellious children subject to God's wrath like everyone else.

But God still loved us with such great love. He is so rich in compassion and mercy. Even when we were dead and doomed in our many sins, he united us into the very life of Christ and saved us by his wonderful grace! He raised us up with Christ the exalted One, and we ascended with him into the glorious perfection and authority of the heavenly realm, for we are now joined as one with Christ!

Throughout the coming ages we will be the visible display of the infinite, limitless riches of his grace and kindness, which was showered upon us in Jesus Christ. For it was only through this wonderful grace that we believed in him. Nothing we did could ever earn this salvation, for it was the gracious gift from God that brought us to Christ! So no one will ever be able to boast, for salvation is never a reward for good works or human striving.

We have become his poetry, a re-created people that will fulfill the destiny he has given each of us, for we are joined to Jesus, the Anointed One. Even before we were born, God planned in advance our

destiny and the good works we would do to fulfill it!
(Ephesians 2:1–10 TPT)

We need to aspire to the unique, personal, and beautiful calling God has given us! An irresistible recipe emerges when we magically combine ingredients and come up with a masterpiece. Here's my instructions for being an everyday hope masterpiece:

1. Refresh under the waterfall of God's presence and peace.
2. Surrender to Spirit _____ (mind, will, body, emotions).
3. Give up any worries and cares (anything that causes heaviness).
4. Experience God's love in a real and personal way.

Every day is new, and every day is different. These ingredients can't be contained in a formula; it's a relationship. We are not a soda machine, where we say the right prayers and then get the necessary result. This is a much more exciting adventure. Walking and talking with Jesus and the Holy Spirit is the best way to live. Sometimes it means making declarations based on our spirit (so much more than positive thinking). Sometimes it means being still and knowing that He is God. Sometimes we may experience His love in the car, while other times we'll be drinking coffee in the kitchen; the only thing that's the same every time is that God's love is personal and real.

 **Life Application**

As you've been aspiring to wake up happy, you've come so far. In part 1, you learned how to live happy. In part 2, you developed the invisible you. And in part 3, you learned how to surrender to the real you. Now you're going to top it all off by living in hope because you're so rich—rich in laughter, peace, and wisdom, and none of these are contingent on other people or any circumstance.

It's time to get practical and find out what it means to live with hope—*real* hope.

To wake up smiling is …

**having confident expectation
and joyful anticipation.**

DAY 32

Living above the Hope Line

One day I was feeling particularly weighed down by a situation with one of my kids. I found myself trying to figure out what I was doing that wasn't working and how I could help. Those thoughts turned into a bit of anger as I wondered what I had done to deserve this. Sure, these types of thoughts are debilitating and on the verge of stupid, but when we're in the middle of it and not being intentional in interrupting our thought patterns, our mind and thoughts take the wheel. It's so easy to turn a corner and travel down that road.

It amazes me how a picture is worth a thousand years. On that particular day, I invited Jesus into my thoughts and confessed, "Lord, I don't have perspective here. I'm feeling hopeless, and it's turning into anger and blaming. I really need your help." I surrendered my thoughts for His thoughts and asked for His way of seeing instead of my limited sight. A picture of a horizontal line on a graph—the hope line—appeared. The Lord had showed me how I have a choice whether I want to live above or below that hope line.

Above the hope line was living in heaven on earth. Thoughts of peace and trust, clear pathways of direction, clear sailing. Below the hope line was like living below the surface of the ocean. Gasping for breath, trying to feel the ground for footing, flailing to get perspective. Below the hope line was living life tossed by the circumstances of a world where kids make their own choices, bank accounts dwindle, health causes concern, and relationships bring drama.

My choice became clear. I had been living above the hope line pretty consistently for several months, living the truths I'd been writing about surrendering to Spirit Audrey, and it had really changed my perspective and my thought life. My faith had grown tremendously. But when this situation happened, out of deep mama-bear love, I wanted to join my child in life. I was willing to go down to a certain level (below the hope line) and experience it as well. I had a noble motive, but it wasn't a good idea.

The Lord showed me that a much wiser move would be to reach below the hope line and invite that child up to join me; I had to resist letting the situation drag me below, which would be counterproductive. Then it was up to my child to choose to grab my hand of help or not. We can't control anyone else's choices. When we as parents or grand-parents step into our kids' situations and bring direction when they aren't asking for it, that's often considered highly unattractive. But simply being a person who lives above the hope line? That's contagious.

I caught the message and declared, "I'm going to remain here above the hope line, completely convinced of God's faithfulness, power, and love. There's no need to control. The present circumstances and present issues and seasons may attempt to force me below the hope line, but the visual of living above it gives me the extra oomph I need to stand firm." I made a choice to line up with heaven and live in hope every day. (That situation with one of our kids has completely turned around, and I'm pretty sure there was a bit of shock as to how easygoing I was with the whole thing!)

And what about the people around us who aren't necessarily as happy? We can continue to live with compassion and empathy, but we don't have to join them in their hopelessness. We are missionaries to our families, and we can nurture the presence of God—and of hope—wherever we go. But we can only do this when we're surrendered to our spirit, which is surrendered to the Holy Spirit. On our own we can never have long-lasting hope.

Those with the most hope will always have the most influence. That's you and me! Feeling weighed down with relationship issues, financial challenges, and health concerns is real life. Over the next few days, we'll look more at the weights that keep us from living above the hope line.

 Life Application

Visualize the hope line in your life. Make an agreement with yourself that you want to live "light," and ask the Holy Spirit to drop into your heart the dream to live above the hope line. It's time to put off the weights that prevent this dream.

To wake up smiling is …

choosing to live above the hope line.

DAY 33

The Weight of Anxiety and Concerns

Every time we choose to carry a concern, we get heavier. It only takes a few cares, and before long we're back living below the hope line, trudging through the ups and downs of circumstances, and tossing to and fro between good days and bad days. Sometimes we live in apprehension of what awaits us in the future. Let's keep in mind that being a lightweight (when it comes to cares and concerns) allows us to abide above the hope line, full of wisdom and clarity of thought, fulfilled by peace and joy.

The offspring of fear is hopelessness. When we embrace fear, we lose sight of the tools and the amazing hope we have in God. We carry the weight of the fear and drop below the hope line, suddenly feeling completely abandoned and that there's no answer for our situation. We've done everything we know to do, and we forget the many things God has already done for us.

The crazy thing about fear and anxiety is that it causes

us to lose sight of the access we have to the answer from God. It's like a heart blocker; we can't seem to remember one good thing He has done or one prayer He has answered. But no matter what fear wants to tell us, we do have a history with God.

> Come and show me your mercy,
> as you do for all who love your name.
> Guide my steps by your word,
> so I will not be overcome by evil.
> (Psalm 119:132–133)

As believers in the Lord, it is our continual journey to walk in His footsteps and not be dismayed by the unknowns of the future, or distracted by the pressures of this world. Throughout the Gospels, Jesus teaches us how to live and think, and Scripture makes it clear that we aren't meant to carry this extra weight. In Matthew 11:28, Jesus invites us to come home to Him (above the hope line) when we are "weary and carry heavy burdens," so He can give us rest. The weight of anxiety, worry, and concern for what's to come affects all of us. When we become full of cares, the heaviness makes us care-full. We can only survive so long when we're bearing so much anxiety that we want to control the situation or quit—just fix it or run away. This can result in us becoming care-less, which is dangerous ground where our heart can become hardened to God's presence. Our invitation to "give our worries and cares to God" and live above the hope line is to become care-free.

So why is it that I accommodate fear of the future and even doubt the Lord will continue to lead me? Why do I wake up determined to make a great plan for my day and also keep at the forefront of my mind my "well-thought-out mission statement" coupled with carefully timed goals and to-do lists? Well, probably because it's a good idea to do that and I enjoy fulfilling purpose for each day. However, our plans are many, but God's purposes prevail. In other words, it's important to humbly ask God for direction each day, and to never forget the best things in life aren't always planned but are given to us as a gift from our Dad in heaven. He made plans and created tasks for us to accomplish before the foundations of the earth were even laid.

It's your day, my precious friend. You don't have to carry your concerns for one more day. You can give them to Him because He cares that much about you. The benefits of living this lifestyle are more amazing than many people ever imagine.

 Life Application

Identify the worries and cares you have been holding on to. As a tangible act, simply take your fist and hold that care tightly. As you look at your fist and imagine the person or situation that has been causing anxiety in your heart, ask yourself, Do I really need to carry this concern, or is God big enough that I can trust Him with it? Pause, and when you feel ready, speak to that anxiety, saying, "I don't want you. I don't need you. I've been carrying you for a while and it feels like you're part of me, but you're not benefitting my life. I send you away." Then imagine that care floating far away and Jesus saying, *I can take care of this*. Now thank the Lord for the blanket of peace that melts away the residue of that long-carried concern that so affected your life.

You may have to do this many times, every time that concern wants to come back. Don't get discouraged; just repeat the exercise. You're writing new realities on your heart as you're trusting your Father in heaven like never before.

To wake up smiling is …
daily giving my cares to Him.

The Weight of Unanswered Prayer

Unanswered prayer results in huge disappointment and can wreak havoc when it comes to hope. We think, *If God is so faithful and loving, why didn't He answer my prayer in my desperation? How could He turn a deaf ear to my cry for help?* In the book of Psalms, David asked these questions over and over when his very life depended on it.

I remember the days following the discovery that I was pregnant as the result of the affair I had. I was broken, repentant, forlorn, and destitute, with no hope. I couldn't bear the thought of a baby who didn't look like my other children, and I couldn't face the future. I remember praying, "God, if I've ever asked you for anything in my whole life, please, please, please hear my heart. I'm begging you to forgive me, begging for a miscarriage. Please take this baby from me." He didn't answer my prayer.

There are much more noble cases than mine. Maybe you've prayed for healing for a loved one, protection from tragedy, or salvation for family members. The list could go on and on. The first reason He doesn't answer our prayer is that He has given us free choice. He says to us, *I can pursue people with my love, but love never controls or forces acceptance.* Oh, how He cries with us at our loved ones refusing to accept Him.

The second reason is we have already presumed the best way for Him to do it. In my case, I couldn't be more grateful (to the point of tears every time I think about it) that He saved our son's life from my choosing abortion or from a miscarriage. I would've missed one of the most beautiful gifts I've ever been given.

A great biblical story is that of the Israelites leaving Egypt with the dream of the Promised Land. There are precious, wise lessons to be learned from our forefathers, and this story is such a prophetic picture of our present circumstances. Just like Moses and the Israelites, we are choosing to live above the hope line and refusing to abide with the weight of fear, shame, worry, rejection, and bondage. Above the hope line is the promised land of safety, love, freedom, and peace.

It's easy for us to judge the Israelites and say, "Come on, people. Stop going around and around in circles in the wilderness. Can't you see the Promised Land right in front of you?" We can easily evaluate the situation and offer a solution because we know what happens; we see the entire picture. Well, what a concept! That's exactly what our loving Father could say about our lives. He sees the big picture and knows the entire story of our lives.

The challenge was that the Israelites had to deal with the limiting beliefs in their hearts. Our entire life story is the outcome of what we truly believe in our heart. We may have the "right" conscious beliefs in our mind, but getting to the deepest place of our heart is a different journey—and while He can't do *for* us, He very much wants to do it *with* us. As we throw off the weights of disappointment, He writes truth on our heart.

God saw the great big picture in the Israelite's story, and out of His heart of love, He could foresee the future. If the Israelites had gone straight to the Promised Land without turning right or left, their next step would have been to overcome the inhabitants (the enemy giants) and take the land for themselves. God knew while they were equipped with the *skills* to win, they didn't have the *heart* to win. So He basically said, *I'm going to take them the long way around, because if I take them there immediately, their hearts will be afraid and they'll go right back to Egypt.*

God doesn't want us to be afraid, and He doesn't want us to go running back to slavery when He has placed freedom within our grasp.

God creates detours around battles you're not ready and equipped to win. This is so important to know about His love for you! Even if God doesn't answer your exact prayer or deliver you from a situation, He has complete confidence in your story, and He has prepared victory for your future, even if you can't see it right this minute. What an encouraging and beautiful nugget of wisdom this brings to your current situation. Your Dad desires to benefit your life. Believe it!

Pray this prayer with me: *Father, the opposite of disappointment is unexpected pleasure. I take this cloak of disappointment caused by unanswered prayer, and I replace it with a beautiful new garment of hope for the future. You can see my life story from beginning to end, so I'm going to trust you. I will no longer presume that I know the best way for you to answer my prayer. You are faithful. You never disappoint. You are committed to my future. You are the God who answers prayer. In Jesus' name, amen.*

To wake up smiling is …
anticipating unexpected pleasures.

DAY 35

The Weight of an Offense

Holding an offense is one of the weights that will definitely keep us from living above the hope line: "Make allowance for each other's faults, and forgive anyone who offends you. Remember, the Lord forgave you, so you must forgive others" (Colossians 3:13).

Have you ever felt like it's impossible to forgive someone? We live in a fallen world, and chances are good that we've all had something said or done to us that never should have happened. If we find ourselves dwelling on this terrible thing, it's time to forgive—really forgive once and for all—and be free from the offense that is limiting us! But how?

Many people carry bitterness to some degree, and it's robbing us of ultimate health, extraordinary relationships, true joy, and the ability to laugh easily and live in peace. But it doesn't have to be that way. We can live life free—completely liberated from the offenses that have crippled us.

When our worth has been violated, we experience anger and resentment. The words or abuse become a barrier between us and the other person, and the relationship is fractured. Even if we want to, we can't live as though the wrong hasn't been done. Something inside of us calls for justice. This is a human reality. Justice may bring temporary satisfaction, but it can't restore relationship. There's nothing easy about sending an offense away, but there's also never been a better day to make that decision and choose freedom and unconditional love.

The weight of anger is exhausting to carry. We all have our buttons, and they're personal and different for each person. A few years ago, a great big button got pushed when people prospered and seemingly got super successful even though they weren't living a life of integrity and honor. Justice in me wanted to scream, *This isn't fair!* and the unredeemed, prideful, carnal-natured me said, *You don't deserve to look so good to this world! You're lying and holding secrets!*

Paul writes, "And 'don't sin by letting anger control you.' Don't let the sun go down while you are still angry, for anger gives a foothold to the devil" (Ephesians 4:26–27).

How does anger enter our homes and relationships and have so much power over us? Anger is a fruit of a deeper problem, or, more accurately said, the sign of buried pain. Every person has the need to feel safe, loved, and valued. Negative experiences and hurtful words damage our hearts, and out of the fear of being rejected and unloved, by default we succumb to anger and even rage. Fear will always seek to control, and anger is a weapon of control. So how do we get to the root of fear leading to anger? The answer is always love. As love heals a broken heart, there is no more room for fear.

🌺 Life Application

People have mistreated you and subsequently influenced your life, and there is most likely residue of pain that still affects you. So, the most practical question you can ask yourself is, How long will I let the people who mistreated me influence my life? And, how much longer will I continue giving them a permanent place in my life and future?

Think about Jesus's forgiveness. He forgave without us asking Him to, and He forgave us permanently. Forgive the same way Jesus did. Take away the power of the wrong done to you by repeating this: "I won't sin by letting anger control me. I won't let the sun go down while I'm still angry, for anger gives a foothold to _____" (put the name of the person/offense in the blank). Today is your day to seize the moment and finally be done with the offense that has been permeating your thoughts. Say to the offense, "I don't want you. I don't need you. You are not benefitting my life. I send you away!"

Today is a great day for freedom. The weight of the offense is gone, and you are able to live effortlessly above the hope line.

To wake up smiling is …
being free from any offense.

The Weight of Regrets, Guilt, and Secrets

I encourage all of us to "put off" the extra weight of regrets, shame, and secrets. It's time to fully receive the washing flood of forgiveness that Jesus paid for when He died and rose again. Regrets will prevent us from being thankful, and they will weigh us down and keep us from living above the hope line. I fully understand the thoughts of wishing we had made different choices, but it's too late for that now. Stop the self-judgment and the continual why questioning, and begin asking, what now?

My parents are in their late seventies, and their love for people and for God has been a living example for me to aspire to. In the last few years, I've really appreciated the pact they've made with each other: "We won't look back unless it makes us smile." There will always be things we would have changed and pain we could have prevented, had we only made a better choice. But when we're washed completely clean, clothed in the righteousness of Jesus our faithful King, we can leave the past behind us and charge ahead to gain anything and everything Jesus has planned for our future.

Another weight we carry is guilt from our poor choices and past failures. The fact that we sinned is an indicator that we believed we would benefit in some way to receive pleasure, escape, or revenge. The truth is that sin always leads to pain and ultimately death. The writer of Hebrews reminds us:

> Therefore, since we are surrounded by such a huge crowd of witnesses to the life of faith, let us strip off every weight that slows us down, especially the sin that so easily trips us up. And let us run with endurance the race God has set before us. (12:1)

Worries and cares of this world show themselves in our thoughts as guilt, unresolved conflict, and selfishness. I love the Scripture in Hebrews where we are in the midst of a race called the life of faith, and it just isn't smart to get slowed down by sin that so easily trips us up. It's virtually impossible to be aware of our own selfish behavior. Unless it is all-out blatantly rude behavior, selfishness is super sneaky.

Scripture so clearly promises us that when we confess to God and ask Him for forgiveness, He is faithful and just to forgive us of our sins (1 John 1:9). However, sometimes we need to go the next step and confess our sins to another person. I'm not saying we have to tell the whole world about our worst mistake, but the Bible does tell us to confess our sins one to another and we'll be healed (James 5:16). There's a healing that takes place when we release a secret from the dark place of our heart and tell someone; the power of that secret is broken. So, if you're holding a secret, I encourage you to find someone you trust and share it. The Holy Spirit will lead you with wisdom, and He wants you to feel loved and accepted despite anything you've participated in.

Living above the hope line is taking off the weights of secrets, unconfessed sin, guilt, and regrets. Ask God to baptize you with the Holy Spirit. In Scripture, the Holy Spirit is often associated with wine. Just as people who drink a little wine are able to smile easier and don't care as much about what people think of them, those who drink the wine of the Holy Spirit become free from caring about past mistakes, the pressures of this world, and any guilt that others want to put on them.

Paul prayed for the Romans: "I pray that God, the source of all hope, will infuse your lives with an abundance of joy and peace in the midst of your faith so that your hope will overflow through the power of the Holy Spirit" (15:13 VOICE).

 ## Life Application

Put off and send away the regrets that haunt you (name them), the sins that entangle you (name them), the guilt that people put on you (name what it is), and the secrets that you have kept in darkness. Put on peace, righteousness, forgiveness, cleansing, and complete acceptance. Forgive yourself as you receive the beautiful gift of forgiveness from Jesus.

Leaving your old life behind means refusing—literally refusing—to let the enemy remind you of your mistakes or your former misery. Today is the perfect day to draw that line in the sand and shout from the housetops, "I am forgiven, I am free, and God has promised me gladness in proportion to my former misery!"

To wake up smiling is …

only looking back when it makes me smile.

The Truth about Wanting to Give Up

True confession: there have been seasons in my life when I wanted to throw in the towel. And by that, I mean somehow escape this pressure-cooker culture of bills, taxes, ministry, money, and social media, and get myself to a beach and learn to play guitar. I'm sure you get the picture. Sing for a meal, talk to people who will stop and listen, and just smile at the sunset each night.

It all sounds sweet and serene, but you do realize I'm describing a homeless person, don't you?

Being overwhelmed with the demands of this world is something most every person faces—but not the childlike ones. Every child's dream is to have a warm home with loving and caring parents. Children who have that don't feel overwhelmed. Nothing has changed. I still want a warm home and to be taken care of, and if I can just get perspective about my heavenly Father again, I won't be overwhelmed. That's literally all it takes.

The choice in front of me is simply this: Do I want to work hard to be a clever, tenacious, respected winner in this world … or do I want to be a child of God who absolutely knows my identity and rests in Dad's security? As soon as I take it upon myself to be a conquering champion in my own right, I get overwhelmed. But when I take a deep breath and remember who I am and *whose* I am, together we face the day and I wake up smiling.

During one of my desire-to-escape seasons, I didn't feel adequate enough to live a successful life. I didn't feel like I was capable of things that are important in our culture, like social networking and marketing, and I believed that if I was truly going to influence people, I had to not only do this and that but also be amazing at it. Sheesh, it just got to be too much.

So I plopped down in my backyard and stared at the sky.

After a few moments, I heard the whisper of the Lord in my heart: *Audrey, do you want to know why I made you?*

Instantly, I thought, *Ah, yes. That would be nice at this point.*

I heard the words, *I made you to love and celebrate. Love people with my love and celebrate me and celebrate life.*

I thought, *Do you know how easy that is? Loving and celebrating are the easiest things in the world for me to do.*

I have gone back to that moment many times since, just to remind myself of my original design. You see, there is a reason God made you too. It's unique and personal, and it's something that comes easy; it's God's redemptive purpose for making you. Don't worry yourself into a tizzy trying to be amazing at everything, and don't beat yourself up when you're not. Instead, rest in His purpose for you. The best things in my life have been the ones I didn't dream up. They just happened when I was doing ordinary life with my extraordinary God.

God's purpose for your life will take place. It's a slow-moving force so powerful that nothing that can stop it. Sometimes humans make elaborate plans and stupid mistakes, but God in His creative strategy is able to continue the force of purpose in you so that nothing in this life can shake it. Love and celebrate until the day you see Jesus face-to-face.

Life Application

What comes easily and naturally to you? What do you do in life that is effortless—that would happen even if you weren't trying? God designed you with a beautiful purpose. It's unique, it's personal, and it is going to happen. Thank God for His purposes in you. If you look back, I'm pretty certain you'd see that the best things that have happened to you were things you didn't plan. God's purposes prevailed.

I love *The Voice* translation, where Paul writes: I'm not there yet, nor have I become perfect; but I am charging on to gain anything and everything the Anointed One, Jesus, has in store for me—and nothing will stand in my way because He has grabbed me and won't let me go.

Brothers and sisters, as I said, I know I have not arrived; but there's one thing I am doing: I'm leaving my old life behind, putting everything on the line for this mission. I am sprinting toward the only goal that counts: to cross the line, to win the prize, and to hear God's call to resurrection life found exclusively in Jesus the Anointed. (Philippians 3:12–14)

To wake up smiling is …

**serving others because
I know who I am.**

DAY 38

The Truth about Hard Times

How can we live above the hope line when bad things happen? Can we presume that God is actually allowing accidents to take place to teach us a lesson? Or could it be that the enemy is scared of our effectiveness and is attacking us with horrible circumstances?

These thought patterns indicate we are in need of a paradigm shift when it comes to our God concept. Christians throughout the generations have "blamed" God for bad things happening, thinking He is the Great Judge ready to punish us for our imperfections. Others have given a large amount of power to satan, presuming he is scheming against us through accidents, falling stock markets, or bad investments.

The truth is God is our protector, our provider, and our promoter. The enemy is the accuser, and he lies to us through the thoughts in our mind and the beliefs of our heart. We live in an imperfect sin-infested world where

accidents, economic downfalls, sickness, and death all happen. But because Jesus Christ has chosen to make His home
in my heart, I can (very intentionally) receive His promises and refuse to let fear or worry of "bad things" rule my
thought life.

So, what do we do about the tough unanswerable questions in our heart? Can we really just choose to live "light"
above the hope line while still living in reality? James tells
us, "If any of you is deficient in wisdom, let him ask of the
giving God [who gives] to everyone liberally and ungrudg-
ingly, without reproaching or faultfinding, and it will be
given him" (James 1:5 AMPCE).

What a marvelous invitation from Almighty God! Spend
a little bit of time meditating on this great Scripture. Our
Father gives us an open invitation to ask for wisdom, and
He guarantees He'll impart it to us without any reservation.
This should bring joy and confidence to our heart.

So why is it that we, as God's children, sometimes doubt
whether our prayers have been heard and answered? Because
we allow discouragement, doubt, and fear to take over. Once
I was fighting a flu bug for a few days, and coupled with a
few hormonal issues, in my weakness I began to feel overwhelmed by the future and simply tired of "fighting the good
fight." I was tempted to curl up in a ball under my covers and
hope the world would go on without me, which I did do for
several hours, but I knew I couldn't stay there. I was simply
going through a hard time.

I confessed my weakness to the Lord and thanked Him

for the truth—that when I am weak, He is strong. I fought through feelings and quoted Scripture all day long, and I prayed in the Spirit and declared that I walk by faith and not by sight. It wasn't fun, and I didn't "feel" victorious, but how can I encourage others to do this if I don't do it myself? It is possible to discipline ourselves back into hope. We can declare God's goodness when we feel nothing but despair, and we can thank God for the fuel of joy to fill up our tank.

We all get opportunities to ask God for wisdom and then fight through the fog of discouragement and doubt. The beautiful reality is that He meets us there and we begin to see the light in midst of the storm. He loves it when we ask, and it pleases Him when we know our need for Him.

Life Application

Pray this prayer during the hard times: *Father, all of your promises belong to me. You are the sovereign God who works on my behalf. I don't know how this will work out, but you do. It's an offering. The Bible calls this strength and fruitfulness. I'm engaging my life into your reality above the hope line. I'm taking this lie that the enemy is trying to isolate to bring destruction and loss, and I join it with fruitfulness and strength. I am taking a moment in the middle of this contrary circumstance and I will exalt you!*

When you do this, you're prophesying over the details of your life. You will be fruitful, you will have strength, you will be bountiful, you will prosper, and you will become whole. Your heart is now focused on Him instead of the problem. It's amazing how when you exalt His kindness, He releases power to deal with the obstacles. You delight in Him, and He fixes things for you. Things start turning around—not always in a moment, and sometimes in a season—but you can trust Him.

To wake up smiling is ...

prophesying to my current circumstances and delighting in Him.

DAY 39

Oh, to Be a Prisoner

R eturn to your fortress, you prisoners of hope," writes the prophet Zechariah; "even now I announce that I will restore twice as much to you" (9:12 NIV). God is inviting us to return to His fortress—His safe place where there is strength and strategy. Then He names us (did He just say *prisoners?*).

I find nothing appealing about being called a prisoner or experiencing the torture of being trapped and held in confinement. Freedom and living in spacious places sound so much better. I don't want any ball and chain of fear or lies to limit me from loving life; I want to be free to love and free to dance. Any concept of being a prisoner to anybody or anything is not my jam—that is, until this hope-filled amazing Scripture in Zechariah comes to my attention.

Can you imagine being a prisoner of hope? I love visuals, so imagine this with me: There's an immovable ball and chain around you called hope, and you can't seem to escape. It holds you captive to live life above the hope line. Thoughts of "reality" seek to remind you that you have no business having so much hope. Circumstances happen in life, and there's no reason to have hope, but you just can't help yourself. You're a prisoner to this hope, and you can't leave it no matter how tough things get. Hope is your very life. Jesus in you is your fortress, and there is never a need to revert to despair.

Accuse me of radical hope all you want, but I am a prisoner to this reality. Our culture defines hope as wishful thinking, but this goes much deeper. For a child of God, hope is a joyful anticipation of God's goodness and faithfulness. Hope is when I'm celebrating something before it even happens. It's easy to have hope when things are looking fabulous, but true hope begins when opposition is staring me in the face.

The enemy loves to lie and use thoughts in our head, saying things like, *How can you even dare to believe that this is going to turn around?* But I respond aloud, "I don't know when it's going to happen, but believe me, there will be breakthrough. It might be today, it might be next week, or it might be in five years, but let me tell you about my Dad. Not only is He powerful and mighty, but there is also nothing He can't do. He is the Creator and King of this universe. Even more importantly, there's nothing He won't do for me."

Return to your fortress and safe place, you prisoner of hope. Any area of your life for which you have no hope is under the influence of a lie. Sometimes people become careless or lazy in their faith, and they allow parts of their life to have no hope. It seems like they're fine and strong in some areas, but when it comes to this one particular area … well, they don't want to talk about it. If that's the case for you, it's worth getting to the bottom of the issue and finding the lie. There is no situation that is hidden from the Lord, and He desires to invade your heart and life with hope like never before.

 ## Life Application

If you're lacking hope, ask God to identify the lie that is influencing your life and robbing you of peace and joy, and anticipate His answer. The circumstances may be saying one thing, but you're firmly bound to the realities of heaven.

When God made his promise to Abraham, he backed it to the hilt, putting his own reputation on the line. He said, "I promise that I'll bless you with everything I have—bless and bless and bless!" Abraham stuck it out and got everything that had been promised to him. When people make promises, they guarantee them by appeal to some authority above them so that if there is any question that they'll make good on the promise, the authority will back them up. When God wanted to guarantee his promises, he gave his word, a rock-solid guarantee—God *can't* break his word. And because his word cannot change, the promise is likewise unchangeable.

We who have run for our very lives to God have every reason to grab the promised hope with both hands and never let go. It's an unbreakable spiritual lifeline, reaching past all appearances right to the very presence of God where Jesus, running on ahead of us, has taken up his permanent post as high priest for us, in the order of Melchizedek. (Hebrews 6:18–20 MSG)

To wake up smiling is …
being relentlessly bound to hope.

Hope for True Rest

One morning I took our dog, Winston, for a "solitude" hike on a mountain in the desert. I brought plenty of water for both of us and figured I had thought of everything. But there's something about going uphill in 82-degree weather with no shade that just wipes you out. About halfway to the top, I decided that we'd had enough. Disappointed about not completing our adventure, I sat down on the ground, poured some water for Winston, and settled into defeat.

After a short rest, however, something changed. A shift took place, and because of the rest, I suddenly had a new lease on this hike and was ready to push through to the adventure of getting to the top. A spiritual truth then hit me. Sometimes we feel like we're experiencing exhaustion in a dry place, and it's natural to want to settle into the defeat and just go back. But this is not the time to make a decision. Rather, it is simply the perfect time to *rest*—drink in the nourishment of God's presence and invite the peace of Jesus to be perfect in our heart. Rest will give us new perspective, and rest will bring space to be still and know He is God.

One aspect of the wilderness I've learned from experience is that, generally speaking, the "rains" (the external manifestations and blessings of God's Spirit) dry up. In a natural wilderness, the water to live by comes from deep within the earth, not from the skies. So, if we're looking for external manifestations alone, or even primarily, we will not survive in the wilderness.

In the church today, there's a huge emphasis on the outward manifestations of the Holy Spirit and the manifest presence of God, but not much on the indwelling life of the Spirit and the hidden presence of God. We need both, but the foremost, constant source of life is the indwelling of Jesus Christ. Rains come and go, but the well never runs dry. Winds come and go, but the breath sustains life. If we primarily focus on the outward, we'll need to run from one experience to another, and will have little sustaining power in between. Our walk will increasingly be measured by our present spiritual feelings and experiences.

We must learn to draw from the well of living water that is within us, and live off the indwelling life of Christ. This is an endless, ever-available, accessible source of life that we can draw on simply by turning to the Lord in our spirit and communing with Him there. We can go a long way without the external manifestations if we learn to live by His indwelling life.

Life Application

Perhaps you've been feeling like you're climbing a mountain in the desert—not physically like I was, but emotionally or spiritually. Today is your day to remember that God is at work in you. Don't despair. No matter what the circumstances you're facing, He has an incredible plan for your life. Trust Him and rest in Him.

> For I am about to do something new.
> See, I have already begun! Do you not see it?
> I will make a pathway through the wilderness.
> I will create rivers in the dry wasteland. (Isaiah 43:19)

God is doing great things in your heart, creating a river of peace, joy, and hope to drench your driest places. Open your heart to receive it. He's about to do something new, and He's already begun.

Be blessed, my friend, and wake up smiling.

To wake up smiling is …

**being confident that He who began
a good work in me
is faithful to complete it.**

Acknowledgments

I can't say enough heartfelt words to thank BroadStreet Publishing Group. First of all, for providing all of us with *The Passion Translation* of the Bible! In the last two years, the Scriptures have saturated my heart like never before as Brian Simmons has translated words that I have been reading all of my life and made them new with perspective, rich in love, and fresh with applicable wisdom. It is a tremendous honor to be an author among such an exceptional team at Broad-Street. My special thanks to David Sluka for believing in the message of this book and always understanding my heart. My editors Christy Distler and Bill Watkins have managed to keep me grammatically correct without losing my passion and personality. Believe me, that requires loving care and tremendous skill!

My mom and dad *never* put a leash on my joy, creativity, or sheer volume. They always believed in me, exemplified loving others, and *always* "get me." If there were ever to be an actual "Most Loving Parents in the World" trophy, they deserve it hands down. And they're mine.

There is nothing, I repeat nothing, and no one that makes me smile more than our kids. Our "Meisner-Family-Love" group-text-stream is one of my favorite things in each day. So much raw honesty and unconditional love in our relationships. Thank you to Christopher, Janelle, David, Tessa, and Robert for laughing and being silly together. Oh, and for humoring me by constantly playing board games whenever we are all together. (And may I mention that our son David drew every flower on the cover of this book? I guess I just did).

My final thanks go to that love of my life for thirty-three years, my Bob. He just can't help telling me how beautiful I am in all my glory! You are profound. You have always believed in me, and the message and project of this book. We have experienced phenomenal love together, we laugh at the same stupid stuff, and we don't have secrets. I'm a pretty lucky girl to have you. You make me smile.

About the Author

Audrey Meisner is a best-selling author, speaker, TV host of the popular Canadian TV show *My New Day*, and founder of *Love Married Life®*. Written alongside her husband, Bob, their book *Marriage Under Cover* presents the message of God's hope after adultery and has saved thousands of marriages. Audrey's book *Like Yourself, Love Your Life* speaks to true beauty and freedom from shame. Audrey has a doctorate in ministry, and her heartfelt message to women is to combat self-destructive thoughts of regret and shame and receive and display God's unconditional love, forgiveness, and smile on their lives. Together, Bob and Audrey specialize in helping marriages build and maintain phenomenal love. They have four children and live in Phoenix, Arizona. To learn more about Audrey, go to bobandaudrey.com.

BobAndAudrey.com